The Beatles

— ACROSS THE UNIVERSE —

The Beatles

— ACROSS THE UNIVERSE —

JOHN, PAUL, GEORGE & RINGO ON TOUR AND ON STAGE

Andy Neill

© Haynes Publishing, 2009

The right of Andy Neill to be identified as the author of this Work has been asserted
by him in accordance with the Copyright, Designs & Patents Act 1988.

All rights reserved. No part of this publication may be reproduced, stored in a retrieval system or transmitted, in any form or by any
means, electronic, mechanical, photocopying, recording or otherwise, without prior permission in writing from the publisher.

First published in 2009. A catalogue record for this book is available from the British Library

ISBN: 978-1-844258-16-1

Published by Haynes Publishing, Sparkford, Yeovil, Somerset BA22 7JJ, UK
Tel: 01963 442030 Fax: 01963 440001 Int. tel: +44 1963 442030 Int. fax: +44 1963 440001
E-mail: sales@haynes.co.uk Website: www.haynes.co.uk

Haynes North America Inc., 861 Lawrence Drive, Newbury Park, California 91320, USA

All images © Mirrorpix

Creative Director: Kevin Gardner
Design and Artwork: David Wildish
Packaged for Haynes by Green Umbrella Publishing

Printed and bound in the UK by J F Print Ltd., Sparkford, Somerset

Contents

Foreword
by DON SHORT

(Former *Daily Mirror* show business columnist)

For me these wonderful images from the archives of the *Daily Mirror*, depicting the Beatles on the road, evoke many magical moments in a life that I shared with them as show business reporter for the *Mirror*. Pop stars came and went in the early '60s but those of us keeping track on entertainment trends were unprepared for the emergence of this phenomenon with its roots in Liverpool's Cavern Club.

As good fortune would have it, I was slightly ahead of the pack. In June 1963, I became one of the first national newspapermen to report about this new group although the story itself was less than flattering. In Liverpool, at Paul McCartney's 21st birthday party, a drunken John Lennon had beaten up a local deejay named Bob Wooler for suggesting that Lennon was gay after John's recent holiday to Spain with manager Brian Epstein. John apologized for his actions and all might have been forgotten. However, with my curiosity aroused, I paid a swift visit to Liverpool and sensed how this talented group – already with two number one hits to their credit – would cross all barriers into mass stardom.

Shortly after their headline-grabbing appearance on the *Sunday Night At The London Palladium* TV show later that year, I covered a Beatles concert in sedate Cheltenham. Filing my story to the *Mirror* office I used the word "Beatlemania" which a sub-editor in the News Room took from my copy and used as a bold headline. It was the perfect descriptive word to convey the scenes now surrounding the Beatles; one that encompassed the mayhem, the hysteria, the noise, the adulation and beyond

John Lennon . . . he helped to write The Beatles' latest hit tune "From Me to You."

Beatle in brawl says 'Sorry I socked you'

By DON SHORT

GUITARIST John Lennon, 22-year-old leader of The Beatles "pop" group, said last night: "Why did I have to go and punch my best friend?

"I was so high I didn't realise what I was doing."

Then he sent off a telegram apologising to 29-year-old Liverpool "rock" show compere and disc jockey Bob Wooler, who was nursing a black eye, bruised ribs and torn knuckles.

The night before Bob and John were both at a Liverpool party to celebrate the 21st birthday of another of the Beatles, Paul McCartney.

'Booted'

Other "beat" music stars—including members of the Shadows and the Pacemakers—were at the party in Dinas-lane, Huyton, Liverpool, when a fight started.

Yesterday Wooler said: "I don't know why he did it. I was booted in the face. I begged him to stop.

"Finally he was pulled off by other people at the party.

"I have been a friend of the Beatles for a long time. I have often compered shows where

they have appeared. I am terribly upset about this—physically as well as mentally."

Wooler was treated for his injuries in hospital, where he was driven by Mr. Brian Epstein, who has the Beatles under contract.

Epstein said last night: "I did not see the incident. All I did was to drive him to the hospital. I can only hope he gets well soon."

John Lennon, in London with the Beatles last night, said: "I had a great deal to drink at the party and very little to eat.

"By the time this happened I didn't know what I was doing.

"Bob is the last person in the world I would want to have a fight with. I can only hope he realises that I was too far gone to know what I was doing."

One of the men who was at the party said: "I looked out of a window and saw Bob Wooler staggering about with blood all over his face. He was saying: 'Get Brian Epstein.'

"I learned later that John Lennon had attacked Wooler.'

PUNCH-LINE: Lennon helped to write The Beatles' latest hit tune "From Me to You."

The Disc Millionaires —See Centre Pages.

"*We were on tour, in one of those houses, like Doris Day's house or wherever it was we used to stay. And the three of us took [LSD]. Ringo, George and I ... But there were so many reporters, there was like Don Short and that ... We were terrified waiting for him to go, and he wondered why he couldn't come over, and Neil [Aspinall], who had never had [acid] either, had taken it, and he still had to play road manager. We said, 'Go and get rid of Don Short', and he didn't know what to do...*"

John Lennon, *Rolling Stone* interview, December 1970

all, the sheer, nerve-tingling appeal of their music. Beatlemania could have been a medical term to describe an epidemic for an epidemic it surely was. A new sound and a new culture – exciting, exhilarating and mesmerizing – swept across concert stages and into social history.

The *Daily Mirror* quickly recognized the advantages of giving maximum space to the exploits of John, Paul, George and Ringo. I was given a carte blanche assignment of tailing the group, reporting on their activities and so it was that I became embroiled for many months in a cat and mouse game of "find the Beatles".

In the early days Brian Epstein saw the potential and importance of the publicity generated by the *Mirror* with its huge circulation. However, within months and with their fame firmly established, the 'Fab Four' did not have to rely on publicity feeds and so accordingly, my assignments became more tactical and intense. When the Beatles attempted to carry out a project under wraps or tried travelling undercover, they were often stunned by my sudden and uninvited appearance – such as the time I tracked John and George down to Ireland on their "get away from it all" Easter holiday in 1964 by climbing over the wall of Dromoland Castle with a bottle of whisky as my letter of introduction!

The Beatle entourage was close knit. Their road managers, Neil Aspinall and Mal Evans, were a tight-lipped team, too aware of the dire consequences of talking to the press. The group remained curious about my sources – George Harrison was often convinced I had a mole somewhere in the organization – but realizing too many 'leaks' were occurring they changed strategy and decided to get me 'on side'. The stalker now occupied a role that my rivals envied and access to the Beatles home phone numbers was a trump card.

I was privileged to travel with John, Paul, George and Ringo on many of their tours at home and abroad – standing in the wings of concert stages, occupying hotel rooms on the same floor, often dining with them and occasionally sharing a seat in the limo. When Ringo fell sick in the summer of 1964, and a world tour was imminent, the Beatles held a press call at Abbey Road Studios to announce that Jimmy Nicol would help them through until Ringo was well enough to return. At one point, drumsticks were thrust into my hands as I slid into Ringo's seat. At that precise moment I was a Beatle! I tapped on the drums, relishing the taste of fame and fortune. But a minute was enough for George. Holding his hands to his ears in mock horror, he shook his head, saying, "Awful! Stick to the day job, Don."

One of the most spectacular highlights for me was covering the Beatles 1965 American tour – particularly the concert at the mighty Shea Stadium baseball ground in New York. While I stood alongside the podium as the Beatles performed, the stands were packed to capacity with 56,000 people. Helicopters above cast searchlights over the arena, flashbulbs popped from every vantage point and the noise was deafening. Pandemonium on this scale erupted at every concert across America but near disaster came when many youngsters were badly crushed as they attempted to lay siege to the stage at San Francisco's Cow Palace. A police chief later told me it was lucky there were no fatalities.

As their ubiquitous shadow I was also party to other contrasting incidents on that same tour, like the incident described elsewhere when the Beatles were on LSD at their private rented home in Bel Air. Poor Neil was, indeed, assigned to distract me with a drink and a game of pool in the downstairs billiard room. He won the game even though as he later confessed the balls were as big as footballs in his chemically enhanced state.

When travelling, the laconic Lennon would often ease the stress of a journey with his wit and humour. We were flying in a chartered plane to Portland, Oregon when one of the engines caught fire. John spotted a black belch of smoke pouring from the engine and nudged me. "We're on fire, start writing, Don, this could be your last Beatles story." I produced an empty film spool and John took it from me, saying, "Let's write our last messages down and roll our notes into the cartridge. It should be safe if the plane goes down." John scribbled his message on a sheet of my notepaper and all I saw him write was "Goodbye world …" The rest I couldn't decipher as he rolled his message into the spool. As the plane descended we could see fire engines and ambulances lining the tarmac. There were strained faces but no panic. Thankfully the plane landed safely amid cheers and applause from all on board. As everyone hurried to the exits John yelled out: "Beatles and children first!" His humour rarely deserted him. My only regret is that the film spool got lost in the rush to get off that plane.

John enjoyed springing surprises on me – and I on him. In London, a man named Freddie Lennon called me claiming he was John's father. John didn't take too easily to the prospect of a reunion with the old seadog who had abandoned him when he was only a toddler but finally I brought the pair together and they resolved many of their differences although there were several turbulent periods in the reconciliation. Much later I warned John that the word was out that he was being targeted by the drugs squad. At the time he was living with his new partner, Yoko Ono, in a London flat. John heeded my warning and cleaned the place out of anything illegal but they still busted him which caused many headaches for him later in America when trying for his Green Card.

There are some precious personal memories I particularly hold close. Paul and George popped over to my home for dinner one night. My then six-year-old daughter Amanda would not go to bed on time so Paul swept her back to her bedroom and soothed her quietly to sleep with a song. A day or two later the headmistress of the local school telephoned my wife and remarked that my daughter had a vivid imagination because she had written a preposterous essay saying how she had met Paul McCartney. My wife told the headmistress, "Well actually it is true." "Oh" replied the headmistress and without a second thought, said, "Do you think you could get Mr. McCartney to open our school fete on Saturday?"

The memories go on – like John managing to weave my name into the quirky text for his satirical book A *Spaniard In the Works*. "That's fame for you, Don," he quipped as he gave me some sheets of the original manuscript penned on the back of toilet paper. I was even given my own mantra for transcendental meditation by George on the expedition to Rishikesh to meet the mystic Maharishi. George also gave me a signed copy of a spiritual book *Autobiography Of A Yogi* hoping to enlighten my thinking.

The last story I wrote on the Beatles as a group came in April 1970, when the *Mirror*'s front page headline stated the unbelievable: "Paul Quits The Beatles". When the paper hit the streets that morning the news desk was jammed with calls from all over the world. Television and radio stations called in to confirm the story. From the editor's office I received a letter of congratulations on my world scoop but ironically with that story my own ticket to ride had expired.

So many other adventures of life with the Beatles come to mind but they are too long to tell here. Besides, Andy Neill needs the space to complete this riveting book which I hope will become the best-seller it deserves to be.

Don Short
August 2009

PAUL QUITS THE BEATLES

McCartney . . . a deadlock over policy with John Lennon

By DON SHORT

PAUL McCARTNEY has quit the Beatles. The shock news must mean the end of Britain's most famous pop group, which has been idolised by millions the world over for nearly ten years.

Today 28-year-old McCartney will announce his decision, and the reasons for it, in a no-holds-barred statement.

It follows months of strife over policy in Apple, the Beatles' controlling organisation, and an ever-growing rift between McCartney and his songwriting partner, John Lennon.

McCartney and Lennon are rated one of the greatest popular songwriting teams of the century.

But there is little doubt that McCartney's decision will bring it to an end.

Safe

In his statement, which consists of a series of answers to questions, McCartney says:

"I have no future plans to record or appear with The Beatles again. Or to write any more music with John."

Last night the statement was locked up in a safe at Apple headquarters in Savile-row, Mayfair—in the very rooms where the Beatles' break-up began.

The Beatles decided to appoint a "business adviser." Eventually they settled for American Allen Klein.

His appointment was strongly resisted by Paul, who sought the job for his father-in-law, American attorney Lee Eastman.

After a meeting in London Paul was out-voted 3-1 by John, and the other Beatles, George Harrison and Ringo Starr.

In his statement today Paul will say what he feels

'Deeply cut up' after policy row

about it all and his attitudes towards Mr. Klein.

Since the Klein appointment, Paul has refused to go to the Apple offices to work daily.

He kept silent and stayed at his St. John's Wood home with his photographer wife Linda, her daughter Heather, and their own baby Mary. He was obviously deeply cut up.

Close friends tried to pacify John and Paul. But August last year was the last time they were to work together — when they collaborated on the "Abbey Road" album.

One friend said: "The atmosphere is distinctly cool. They do not hate one another. This is just deadlock over policy."

Geniuses

Dick James, managing director of Northern Songs, publishers of the Lennon-McCartney songs, told me:

"It could mean that in competition with each other they will even write greater songs. They are both geniuses—Paul a melodic one and John in an inventive capacity."

There were other elements

that hastened Paul's decision to quit. John Lennon, on his marriage to Yoko Ono, set out on projects of his own. Ringo went into films, and George stepped in as a record producer.

Today McCartney will reveal his own plans for a solo programme.

It will include a full-length film based on the much-loved children's book character Rupert.

Secret

But the very first project is an album of his own compositions.

It is simply called "McCartney" which he not only wrote, but produced entirely himself.

He played every instrument to be heard on the 14 tracks. His wife Linda added vocal harmonies.

The whole operation has been in secret. When the first 200 copies were pressed this week McCartney collected them all from the factory — so they could not be "poached."

By tomorrow hundreds of thousands will be rushed across the world. The first should reach Britain's shops by Monday morning.

Introduction

Like the Dead Sea Scrolls or the Royal Family, the Beatles in print is an industry in itself. As I write, something approaching 500 different titles, ranging from academic studies to scurrilous memoirs, have been published, proving that no other group of popular musicians from the 20th century continues to exert the same level of ongoing fascination at what their urbane publicist Derek Taylor once laconically described as "the longest-running story since the Second World War". While other artists may have sold more records and concert tickets or courted more controversy, the Beatles' unique chemistry of strong image and incredible talent with an uncanny ability to reflect and influence the youth consciousness of the 1960s produced a cultural landmark that continues to resonate with generations born well beyond the Beatles' break-up at the end of the decade.

When assessing their seven years in the public eye the Beatles obviously spent a large amount of that time in the studio, particularly in the later period, crafting a timeless body of work. However, before their breakthrough in 1963, the Beatles' reputation rested on being a *live* band, playing hundreds of gigs around their native Merseyside and in the nightclubs of Hamburg. While millions bought their records, the demand to see the Beatles in person was even greater.

No other group were as constantly photographed – whether it was buying a Mini-Cooper or receiving MBEs. While the Beatles' charisma shone through, no matter how mundane the activity, *Across the Universe: The Beatles on Tour and on Stage* examines the Beatles as a performing group – in particular the Beatlemania years of 1963-1964 when seemingly their every movement made news. As well as the group's changing attitude to fame, the photos also reveal the impact the Beatles had on their public – from Blitz-like scenes with British police and nurses attending overcome fans to scenes of adulation in American streets and stadiums.

Leading the charge to report on this musical and social phenomenon was the *Daily Mirror*, Britain's first and leading tabloid newspaper with a circulation reaching 5 million in the mid-Sixties. With a young readership eager for Beatles-related stories, the *Mirror* obliged with a network of reporters (or "stringers" as they were called) and photographers up and down the British Isles covering the group's exploits, as well as accompanying them on overseas jaunts, most notably their unprecedented success in America in 1964. As staff photographer Alisdair McDonald confirmed: "With the Beatles the pictures always went in the paper. The *Mirror* loved the Beatles. With them we couldn't fail. They sold papers, and the *Mirror* was *the* paper."

The stories were duly printed as they happened, and, after being assigned a job reference number, the relevant negatives and contact strips were then stuffed into plain brown envelopes with date, subject, synopsis, photographer, and total number of shots duly noted in biro and filed into small cardboard boxes at the (now demolished) *Mirror* building overlooking Holborn Circus. In most cases, only one or two images from several rolls of film were used for the article in question – the rest lay dormant or, in some extreme cases, destroyed if they were considered beyond any useful purpose.

When the *Mirror* moved its considerable archives to their present site in Watford in 1994, it was found that a unique collection of thousands of *verité* images relating to a myriad of historical and cultural subjects dating back to the early years of the 20th century had been amassed and largely remained unseen. A generous sampling of the *Mirror*'s Beatles archive first appeared in *The Beatles Files*, a now out-of-print 1998 hardback, published by Bramley Books and put together with care and enthusiasm by Andy Davis, news editor of the now defunct *Beatles Monthly Book*.

Since then, even more material, including the archives of Sunday tabloid the *People*, the *Daily Herald* (Glasgow) and colour transparencies from the Syndication International agency have been added to the Mirrorpix vaults and presented within these pages – for the first time in many cases. The pictures, freshly scanned to modern digital standards, tell their own incredible story of how four fresh-faced Liverpool musicians were transformed from a British pop phenomenon into the world's greatest and best-loved group. It also reveals the less enviable side of fame – how the sheer demands of Beatlemania ate away at their initial enthusiasm. By the time the Beatles embarked on their last tour of America in August 1966, in the wake of John Lennon's controversial misquoted statement about the Beatles being bigger than Jesus, it was clear that the relentless pace with which they operated had to stop.

While this book's title is, of course, taken from a popular Beatles song, it also aptly sums up their omnipresence during the Sixties. If technology had been far enough advanced and the Beatles could have played the cosmos then I'm sure manager Brian Epstein would have tried to accommodate it into their already-bulging schedule. Another possible title could have been "A Train And A Room And A Car And A Room And A Room And A Room", the memorable line uttered by Wilfred Brambell in the Beatles' film A *Hard Day's Night* to reflect the relentless treadmill within their goldfish bowl existence.

No demand or request was considered too great, something which would not be tolerated by today's 21st century megastars, surrounded by large entourages supposedly representing their clients' best interests. It is to the Beatles' lasting credit that they were able to fulfil their obligations with a combination of humour, patience and charm (in the early years, at least) while presenting an outward image that this was no hard day's night but fun, a laugh and all in a day's work for the Fab Four.

It's also to the *Mirror*'s credit that their intrepid reporters and photographers were never far from capturing the phenomenon as it unfolded for a public insatiable in their appetite for the beloved Mop Tops. Here, then, is the best of those images from the stories the paper covered of the Beatles on tour and on stage, as they moved through a more innocent world. To amplify John Lennon's succinct quote when looking back to his '50s youth, "You shoulda been there."

Andy Neill
August 2009

15

The Photographers

Back in the 1960s, the *Daily Mirror* employed around 20 staff photographers (a far greater number than today) and most of them covered the Beatles throughout the decade. Because there was no particular photographer specifically allocated Beatles assignments, a crack team were on hand to capture the Fab Four's movements. Among those whose work is represented in this book are Freddie Cole, Bill Ellmann, Monte Fresco, Kent Gavin, George Greenwell, Curt Gunther, Eric Harlow, Bob Hope, Tom King, Tommy Lea, Charles Ley, Cyril Maitland, Arthur Murray, Charles Owens, Eric Piper, Peter Stubbs, and Bela Zola.

By far, the paper's most prolific Fabs-related smudgers were Victor Crawshaw and Alisdair MacDonald, who both joined the *Mirror* staff on the same day in 1960. Among his duties, Crawshaw was stationed at Heathrow (or London Airport as it was commonly known then) from 1964, while MacDonald was fortunate enough to accompany the Beatles to Paris and America that same year.

"None of us were pop fans", Crawshaw told Andy Davis. "It was just another job, and it was quite hard work. We had excellent cameras. Rolliflexes. Wonderful cameras! But you had to get your focus right – there was no such thing as auto-focus then. We didn't even have exposure meters. You had to get your exposures right according to the film you were using, and you'd have to know that in your head. You wouldn't have time to go and take a light-meter reading, you just knew what the light was and set it."

"[The *Mirror* picture editors] weren't very interested in the Beatles at first," Crawshaw confirms. "The stories weren't so much about them, but what happened around them. We'd mainly stand with our backs to the stage photographing the kids. All the paper wanted to see were these hysterical swooning girls. We'd do two or three pictures of the Beatles and then concentrate on the fans."

"It was hard to get great pictures of the Beatles playing live," said MacDonald, "because the lighting in those days wasn't very good. They would be spread across the stage and, being at the back, Ringo was always hidden behind his drums. So to get a good shot of all four of them to illustrate a story, we'd have to go backstage, before or after a performance.

"There was always a problem photographing the Beatles or any group for that matter, because there were four of them. If you didn't get them several times, one was likely to have his eyes shut, another might be looking the other way or making a funny face. So you took as many frames as you could to get it right. Hotels, taxis, aeroplanes, they were the expenses. Film was the cheapest product. So you didn't skimp. You just banged away."

The Beatles willingness to pose in the contrived but innocent style so favoured by photographers in the early to mid Sixties suggests the group were happy to play ball.

"The Beatles were very good, very funny," MacDonald confirmed, "although I thought John Lennon got pissed off very quickly. He had a short fuse. Paul McCartney could get a bit delicate as well…"

Considering the quality of some of the shots contained herein, none of the *Mirror* pictures were premeditated. "You couldn't set up anything with the Beatles", Crawshaw recalled to Davis. "Absolutely nothing. Everything was taken as you could get it. We used to have to get to the concerts well in advance. I wouldn't say it was a struggle, because the Beatles were there to have their pictures taken, but they wouldn't necessarily stop and hang around for long. You weren't given much time at all. You had to be pretty sharp, otherwise they'd be gone.

"It wasn't usually the Beatles who were the problem, it was the people who surrounded them. They were kept on the go by the police, the managers, the agents. They didn't have the heavies in those days that groups have today, but they still kept them moving."

MacDonald recalls the trip to Paris in January 1964. "[The Beatles] stayed at the George V Hotel while we were in lesser accommodation, along with the rest of Fleet Street and the group didn't come out for ages. We didn't like their press officer, Brian Sommerville, as he was never very helpful to us. But we pushed it and pushed it and finally got them out onto the Champs-Elysées. I got the group to pose looking at some postcards, and while I was taking the pictures George Harrison said, 'We're glad you came along, we'd been dying to get out!' They didn't know we'd been banging on the door. Sommerville didn't want them to peak too early, probably."

MacDonald was witness to the backstage rumpus that occurred at the Olympia involving the French paparazzi. "It's an unwritten rule in France that you always keep the dressing room door open. Being the Beatles, of course, they shut it, and it developed into a fight backstage. You know in the movies how, when someone gets hit over the head with a chair, it breaks into little bits? Well it happened that night in Paris – the bloke went down, but the chair stayed in one piece!"

Stationed at London Airport, Crawshaw witnessed the sometimes incredible number of fans who came to see the

Beatles arriving or departing. "Quite honestly it was a pain in the arse whenever the Beatles came through," he candidly admitted. "It just wasn't straightforward. You'd have all these girls camping out, invading the airport a couple of days before the flight. The police used to try and herd them into specific areas but they'd always hear rumours that something was happening at a different part of the airport and charge off looking for them."

MacDonald witnessed the besotted – and sometimes, obsessive – nature of the Beatles' more fanatical following. "I'd get girls coming up to me saying, 'Have you met the Beatles?' 'Yes', I'd say. 'Who's your favourite?' they'd ask. 'I like them all.' 'Have you actually touched them?' 'Well' I've bumped into them', and as soon as I'd said that they'd start stroking me!"

Once the intensity of Beatlemania began to abate in 1965, so too did the *Mirror's* coverage of the group. "We never saw them much after their success in America," said MacDonald. "Mostly only at the airport… After all that stuff about the Beatles being more popular than Jesus happened in the States, they started getting touchy with us. It was all knocking

stories towards the end. They were getting stressed amongst themselves. The stress came over to us, so everyone started knocking them – they were no longer being helpful to us."

Victor Crawshaw: "The Beatles probably thought they were being hounded, but it was nothing when compared to today. They would really have only been photographed when they were actually doing something or going somewhere. They wouldn't have had photographers camping out, chasing them. When they came through the airport, they knew what they had to do. They were there. We were there. We took the pictures and then they went off. That was the way it was done. We never had any problems with them the way photographers do with present day [stars]. The difference is that in the Sixties, everybody wanted to have their picture taken. Nowadays it is fashionable not to."

This overview first appeared in unabridged form in *The Beatles Files* by Andy Davis (Bramley Books 1998). My deep appreciation goes to Andy for allowing me permission to use his interview quotes with Victor Crawshaw and Alisdair MacDonald.

Before Beatlemania

"The Beatles – causing great excitement in Liverpool, but can they do the same in the rest of the nation?"

Disc Weekly, 5/1/1963

Paul and John watched by Cynthia Powell (left) and friends at the Casbah Club, Liverpool.

A significant meeting at a Liverpool church event on 6th July 1957 is where the Beatles story really begins. For it was on this date that 16-year-old John Lennon met 15-year-old Paul McCartney for the first time at St Peter's parish church fête in Woolton. Paul had been brought along by mutual friend Ivan Vaughan to watch Lennon's skiffle group, the Quarrymen, busk through their brief set that warm summer Saturday afternoon. Although the city was full of similar amateur groups, McCartney was impressed enough to seek an introduction to a mildly inebriated Lennon and his fellow grammar school band mates. The precocious left-hander took a guitar, turned it upside down and demonstrated his mastery of Eddie Cochran's 'Twenty Flight Rock' and Gene Vincent's 'Be-Bop-A-Lula' and was able to show Lennon and friends how to tune a guitar. McCartney left having made an impression, and after a few days of indecision John decided to let Paul join the Quarrymen, resulting in one of the 20th century's greatest song-writing partnerships being formed.

By its very do-it-yourself nature, skiffle was a transient craze, swept away by the onslaught of American rock 'n' roll, and as the various members of the Quarrymen dropped away, Paul suggested that his Liverpool Institute schoolfriend, 15-year-old George Harrison, should join the group. Lennon was initially wary of the age gap between them but he was soon swayed by Harrison's proficiency and, in 1958, George became a member of the Quarrymen, who had started to gain some gigs around Liverpool including the Casbah Coffee Club, in West Derby, owned by Mona Best, whose son, Peter, played drums with a group called the Blackjacks.

John had now left Quarry Bank High School without any

major qualifications and had got a place at Liverpool College of Art where he met his first wife, Cynthia Powell, and an aspiring young artist, Stuart Sutcliffe. When a painting of Stuart's fetched over £60 in a local art contest, John cannily persuaded him to invest in a bass and to join the Quarrymen.

With his moody James Dean look, "Stu" brought a new visual focus to the group and suggested they rename themselves the Beatals as a pun on Buddy Holly's Crickets. However, his rudimentary playing was a handicap, costing the semi-pro group – having amended their name to the Silver Beetles – a valuable break in May 1960 to back Billy Fury on a tour. Instead, Fury's manager, the legendary impresario Larry Parnes, arranged for the group to back Johnny Gentle, a lesser-known singer from his "Parnes, Shilling and Pence" stable of artists, on a ballroom tour of Scotland.

For the nine-day tour, the excitable group changed their names to more colourful stage monikers – Paul became Paul Ramon, George became Carl Harrison (in deference to his rockabilly idol Carl Perkins) while Stu assumed the persona Stu de Stael, after the Russian artist Nicholas de Stael. (Popular legend has it that John became Long John Silver, but Lennon always denied this.) The Silver Beetles were accompanied by an older drummer, Tommy Moore, whose brief

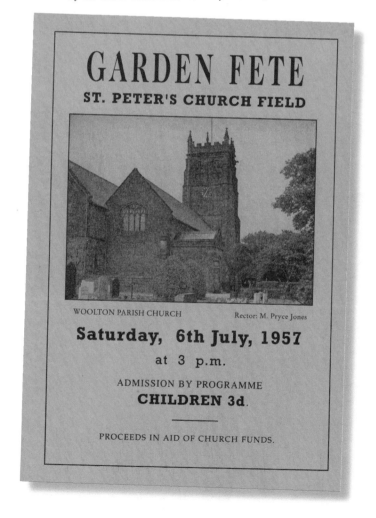

GARDEN FETE
ST. PETER'S CHURCH FIELD

WOOLTON PARISH CHURCH   Rector: M. Pryce Jones

Saturday, 6th July, 1957
at 3 p.m.

ADMISSION BY PROGRAMME
CHILDREN 3d.

PROCEEDS IN AID OF CHURCH FUNDS.

A bearded Ringo Starr drumming with Rory Storm and the Hurricanes.

21

tenure with the future Beatles finished shortly after he was injured in a crash involving the group's van in the Scottish Highlands.

Returning to Liverpool, without a drummer and with another name change to the Silver Beatles, the group continued to play at various dancehalls and youth clubs on Merseyside, often before brawling gangs of feral teenage toughs. They were being managed in a de facto fashion by Liverpool clubowner Allan Williams, and often performed at his coffee bar, the Jacaranda, on Slater Street. "We used to sell jam butties at the Jac," Williams remembered, "and we would charge an extra penny for jam on toast. In those days, [The Beatles] were so hard up that when they came back from a gig, they used to argue as to whether they had enough to cover the additional penny!"

Williams even offered the Silver Beatles work backing a stripper named Janice in one of his short-lived clubs, rather grandly (and misleadingly) named the New Cabaret Artistes, nothing more than an illegal basement shebeen on Upper Parliament Street. Though not the most prestigious of engagements, the nature of the experience was to stand the red-blooded lads in good stead for their next significant career move. Through Williams' endeavours, the Silver Beatles were offered work playing rock 'n' roll in a club in Hamburg, West Germany, throughout the late summer of 1960. However, Williams insisted that a drummer was essential. Until this time the group had skirted around the issue, telling interested parties, "the rhythm's in the guitars".

After visiting their old haunt, the Casbah, Paul approached

Pete Best, offering him the vacant gig. Best readily accepted and the group – now known simply as 'The Beatles' – loaded their gear into Williams' van and headed for Hamburg.

Before arriving the Beatles were just another of the amateurish, semi-professional groups around Liverpool that the impact of rock 'n' roll had thrown up in its wake. In fact, the first of Williams' groups to arrive in Hamburg, Howie Casey, of Derry and the Seniors, had implored Williams not to send over "that bum group, the Beatles", fearing they would spoil the good thing they had going in Hamburg's night spots.

It took three full months for the Beatles to graduate from rank amateurs into a tight, adrenalin-fuelled rock 'n' roll outfit. Thanks to the long hours – up to six-hour stretches over the weekends, firstly at a seedy strip joint, the Indra Club, then, after noise complaints, to the larger, livelier Kaiserkeller further down the Grosse Freiheit – and clubowner Bruno Koschmider's constant exhortations for the group to "Mach Schau" ("make a show"), the Beatles became a totally different proposition to the undistinguished combo they had been when they arrived. Not only had their musicianship tightened up thanks to the demands of the lengthy stage stints that required a varied repertoire, but also they now had three capable vocalists (George had not sung lead before the trip).

The group's self-consciousness evaporated in a haze of beer and pills, with Paul, George and especially John stamping and bouncing like jack-in-the-boxes over the Kaiserkeller's fragile stage, which eventually gave way in a demolition contest between the Beatles and newly arrived fellow Liverpudlian group, Rory Storm and the Hurricanes, whose 20-year-old drummer was a certain Richard Starkey.

However, the Hamburg experience was derailed after an aggrieved Koschmider terminated their contract, having discovered the Beatles' defection to the nearby Top Ten Club, run by rival promoter Peter Eckhorn. Soon afterwards the authorities "somehow" discovered that George was a minor playing in German clubs (the legal age was 18), resulting in his deportation. Struggling on without George, Paul and Pete were arrested for supposedly attempting to burn down their living quarters and were similarly ordered to leave. John had little choice but to follow, arriving home in time for Christmas, while Stu remained behind in Hamburg to study art and spend time with his photographer girlfriend, Astrid Kirchherr, who was part of an unconventional German *exis* movement of artists who had inadvertently stumbled upon and befriended these wild untamed English rockers on the Reeperbahn.

After a week of uncertainty John contacted the others and

Beatles fans outside the Cavern Club, Liverpool.

A rare set of 'The Beatals' signatures
(with Johnny Gentle) signed in Scotland, 1960.

by the time the Beatles made their lunchtime debut at the subterranean venue on 9th February 1961. Like Hamburg, the Cavern became a tremendously important training ground for the Beatles, a place where they could hone their craft, interact with fans and increase their following from Liverpool and beyond. (The Beatles played a total of 292 gigs at the Cavern until their nationwide fame brought the last show there on 3rd August 1963.) The Cavern's DJ was the Beatles' good friend Bob Wooler who helped to obtain many of their early bookings.

As the Beatles' popularity increased, and with longer distances to cover with up to three shows in a day, Neil Aspinall, who had attended the Liverpool Institute with Paul and George, and had been driving the group to and from gigs as a favour for his friend Pete Best, left his post as a trainee accountant to work for the group as full-time road manager. (Aspinall went from loading their meagre equipment into the back of an old Commer van to becoming the Beatles' closest confidante, overseeing their business affairs almost up to his death in 2008.)

As a result of much diplomatic negotiating, and with George now 18, in April the Beatles were allowed to return to Hamburg, where they resumed playing long hours over 13 weeks at Peter Eckhorn's Top Ten Club. One unfortunate consequence was the group's refusal to pay Allan Williams his verbally agreed commission. Williams was understandably less than impressed at how his selfless efforts on the group's behalf had been repaid. It was also during the Beatles' second Hamburg jaunt that they made their first recordings, overseen by orchestra leader Bert Kaempfert for the Polydor label – albeit as a backing group to English singer/guitarist Tony Sheridan, who had been a mainstay of the *Oh Boy!* TV show in England and was now holding down a residency at the Top Ten.

Recorded at a small school, the Beatles were firmly in backing group mode on the songs taped, although they got to record a unique Lennon–Harrison instrumental 'Cry For A Shadow' (its punning title taking a playful dig at the current plethora of British Shadows-inspired outfits performing instrumentals dressed in matching suits with choreographed dance steps) and a solo Lennon vocal on the old 1920s' standard 'Ain't She Sweet'.

With Stuart Sutcliffe's departure from the Beatles now official, Paul McCartney took over full-time bass playing duties (which he had assumed in Sutcliffe's absence). As a proficient guitarist, McCartney's skill on the instrument came as almost second nature, and he would go on to become one of rock's most inventive bassists – a fact sometimes under-

one of the Beatles' first gigs after returning from Germany, was to prove a landmark in their early career. On 27th December, at Litherland Town Hall, the five Beatles (with a friend of Best's, Chas Newby, filling in for Sutcliffe) literally tore the place apart with their wild image, music and antics. The group were billed as being "Direct From Hamburg", so the local kids were astonished to hear the band members' perfect mastery of Scouse.

The Beatles' date sheet quickly filled as a result of the buzz surrounding the Litherland gig, and the group's following swiftly spread around Liverpool's dancehalls and clubs, including the Cavern, on Mathew Street. Previously a jazz club when the Quarrymen had unsuccessfully performed there in 1957, the new owner and promoter, Ray McFall was shrewd enough to sense which way the wind was blowing

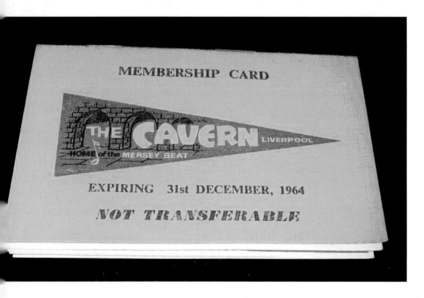

Beatles fans inside the Cavern Club, Liverpool.

acknowledged in the rush to praise his song-writing gifts.

In October 1961 Lennon turned 21 and, thanks to a gift from an aunt, he and McCartney went to Paris where they reconnected with their Hamburg friend, photographer Jürgen Vollmer. Jürgen persuaded the two to wear their hair combed forward like his own, thus giving birth to the Julius Caesar-styled "Beatle haircut". George also adopted the style (some stories suggested it was he who invented the Beatle cut after returning with his hair wet from the swimming baths in Hamburg), but, ominously, the quietly spoken Pete Best refused to change his Tony Curtis-style coiffure.

That same month, a highly fortuitous event occurred when one Raymond Jones entered a Liverpool record store on Whitechapel called NEMS (North End Music Stores) and enquired of the owner Brian Epstein as to whether they had a record made in Germany called 'My Bonnie' by the Beatles. When two other customers made the same enquiry, Epstein was intrigued.

"I always tried to work on the theory that the customer was right," he recalled in 1964. "Eventually I traced the source and ordered some 200 copies of the record… Then I heard that the Beatles were Liverpool boys, had a rapidly growing following and were actually playing in a club near the store…"

The events leading to Brian Epstein becoming the Beatles' manager are well documented. Suffice to say that his arrival

Brian Epstein and George Martin
at EMI Studios, London.

THE BEATLES

PARLOPHONE RECORDS

couldn't have come at a more opportune time, coinciding with the group's growing frustration at being unable to break out of the straitjacket of being kingpins on Merseyside without so much as a look-in to the national scene where, for London's entrepreneurs, they might just as well have been from Mars.

Having no previous experience in managing a pop group, Epstein (or "Eppy" as he became known to the Beatles) set to work with fervour and zeal. He got his charges better-paid gigs and extended these beyond the usual Merseyside radius, insisted the group were punctual and professional and, though facing some initial reluctance, transformed the Beatles' image from leather-clad rock 'n' roll urchins to respectably clad entertainers in proper matching suits and ties. Most importantly, Epstein pledged to scout London to land an elusive recording deal with a major recording company.

When the Beatles were infamously turned down by Decca Records after nervously auditioning at the company's studio on New Year's Day 1962, Brian continued to hawk the rather unrepresentative results of that session to other companies, until a remarkable chain of events in February led to his being formally introduced to George Martin, head of A&R

at Parlophone, the poor relation among EMI's other labels, Columbia and HMV (His Master's Voice) – both of whom had previously turned Epstein down.

George Martin: "Brian Epstein was introduced to me by a mutual friend, Sid Coleman, who worked for Ardmore & Beechwood [a music publishing department subsidiary of EMI]. What had happened was he'd gone in to the HMV shop on Oxford Street to get lacquer discs cut of some of the Beatles' tapes and the engineer heard it and thought they sounded quite interesting. He told Sid, who rang me up and said, 'this guy's been round every record company in London, he's getting nowhere, will you see him?' So I saw him and listened to the tapes which were pretty rough, and I could see why he'd been turned down, but they had something. So I said to Brian bring the boys down to London and I'll give them a [recording] test."

While the Beatles anxiously waited for news as to where their destinies lay, in April they undertook their third Hamburg stint, becoming the first group to play at the newly opened Star-Club for promoter Manfred Weissleder. Unfortunately, a pall was cast over the seven-week season with news of their former comrade

Stuart Sutcliffe's death from a brain haemorrhage, aged only 21. But the gloom was alleviated when a telegram arrived from Epstein in London, reading "Congratulations boys. EMI request recording session. Please rehearse new material."

The Beatles' first session at EMI Studios at 3 Abbey Road, St John's Wood, on 6th June was a success in just about every department. While he was still unconvinced about their musical attributes, Martin was totally won over by the group's "all for one" attitude, charisma and significantly, their humour. The Beatles, in turn, were impressed at Martin having previously recorded their comic heroes Peter Sellers and Spike Milligan. It was to prove a perfect professional and personal partnership. The one snag was Martin's doubt over Pete Best's drumming abilities.

George Martin: "I said to Brian, 'you can do what you like with him [Best] on stage but for the records, I'll be using a session drummer.' It turns out the boys were having second thoughts about Pete anyway."

And so came into being the most underhand action in the Beatles' history: the dismissal of Pete Best, carried out in secrecy rather than being handled face to face by John, Paul and George, who left their hapless manager to do their dirty work.

The move to put Pete out and bring in Hamburg buddy Ringo Starr was not taken lightly by the Beatles' local supporters, since Best had proved the hot favourite among their fervent female following. During the Beatles' earliest existing television footage, filmed at the Cavern for Granada Television on 22nd August during one of Ringo's first gigs with the Beatles, a cry of "Bring back Pete!" can clearly be heard from a disgruntled patron, while George Harrison sports a black eye (it was he who was the most in favour of getting Starr into the group) in a publicity photo session taken at EMI Studios where the Beatles recorded their first single, 'Love Me Do', on 4th September. (Martin, who was unaware of the new drummer's abilities, had a session man, Andy White, on standby for a further 'Love Me Do' session on 11th September, but it is Ringo's drumming that adorns the original single.)

Released on 5th October, 'Love Me Do' entered the *New Record Mirror* chart at 49 and took a zig-zag route in the

business establishment came when they were booked onto their first package tour around Britain's cinemas and theatres, billed below teen sensation Helen Shapiro and pop singer Kenny Lynch. Also on the tour were Danny Williams, the Kestrels, the Honeys, the Red Price Combo and compere/comedian Dave Allen. However, it soon became apparent that many had come to see this new group from Liverpool, and they were moved up in stature to close the first half.

By the time the tour finished on 3rd March, and thanks to important national exposure on television and radio, the Beatles had achieved what producer George Martin had predicted – their first No. 1 single (on the *New Musical Express* chart) with 'Please Please Me'.

Record Mirror described the Beatles as being "hotter than anyone else on the British music scene". In the *New Musical Express* annual readers' poll, despite their status as relative newcomers, the group rated fifth in the World Vocal Group section. On 11th February the Beatles famously recorded their first album, *Please Please Me*, in a remarkably productive day, and on 5th March taped their third single (and second No. 1), 'From Me To You', released on 12th April.

Promoter Arthur Howes had already booked the group onto another package tour – this time with visiting singers Chris Montez and Tommy Roe. The group outshone the American headliners night after night, and to their initial embarrassment but obvious delight went from closing the first half to topping the bill. The same occurred on a bill-sharing tour with Roy Orbison (supported by Gerry and the Pacemakers) in early summer where scenes that were to become a familiarity first manifested themselves, with mobbings becoming a regular occurrence at hotels and stage doors. As the Beatles' success and commitments grew, the diehard Cavern regulars – some of whom would queue overnight in freezing temperatures to get a front row position – realized that the Beatles were Liverpool's exclusive property no longer.

In May, while 'From Me To You' was at No. 1, Polydor cashed in by re-releasing 'My Bonnie', changing the Beat Brothers credit to the more sales-friendly Beatles. As an indication of how much their popularity was snowballing, even this mediocre recording managed a *Record Retailer* Top 50 position for one week. Released in July, the *Twist And Shout* EP went on to achieve sales in excess of 250,000, shattering the EP sales record previously held by Elvis Presley with *Kid Galahad* and outselling most of the singles in the Top 10, while the *Please Please Me* LP sold over 150,000. Publicity photos appeared, taken by Dezo Hoffman, of the Beatles wearing the familiar grey Pierre Cardin collarless jackets that John and Paul

charts before eventually getting to No. 17 for a week. It was enough to renew Martin's faith in the group's potential to release another Lennon–McCartney original, 'Please Please Me' as the follow-up on 11th January 1963.

In December the Beatles played their fifth and final engagement in Hamburg, again at the Star-Club. The demands of playing hours of music night after night in seedy Reeperbahn bars and dives had undoubtedly instilled in them the stamina to handle the pressures which the ensuing years would bring – but now they had outgrown the experience and were eager to return home to capitalize on the success of 'Love Me Do', which had finally entered the Top 20, selling 100,000 copies in total.

"Of course it didn't happen as quickly as it takes to talk about," George told Beatles' ghost-writer Peter Jones. "It's hard to describe the little day-to-day excitements we had all around this time. Every jump in the charts was like a shot in the arm. Honestly, the first time I heard 'Love Me Do' plugged on the radio, I went all shivery and cold."

After starting the New Year by playing several dates in snowbound Scotland during the worst winter in years, the Beatles' first significant step towards joining the show

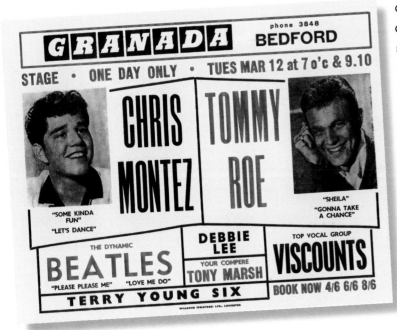

had first seen in Paris in 1961. Within a few months they would be mass-marketed as the "Beatle Suit".

With the Beatles and their Epstein-managed contemporaries Gerry and the Pacemakers and Billy J. Kramer and the Dakotas dominating the British hit parade, along with other Merseyside contemporaries such as the Searchers, an army of A&R men from various London record companies descended on Liverpool like locusts in the hope of landing the next big one, leading to the media coining terms like "Merseybeat" and "The Liverpool Sound" – something that the Beatles were understandably keen to distance themselves from. However, they were undoubtedly the focal point of the new wave of northern groups – a fact well documented in an excellent BBC TV documentary *The Mersey Sound*, filmed in August, where the four individuals came across as intelligent and well adjusted with regard to their new-found fame. It was also becoming rapidly apparent that the Beatles' stage act was being rendered virtually inaudible thanks to a non-stop barrage of screaming from their largely female audience. By the end of the year, the group were resigned to being seen but not heard.

The Beatles had no time to stop and take in their escalating popularity. Even this early success was having its down sides – the constant screaming meant that they could barely hear themselves play, which severely hampered their ability to improve as musicians. In addition, the crowd scenes were now restricting their access to the outside world, and after a rash remark made by George indicating that jelly babies were his favourite sweet, for the next year or more

the Beatles had to dodge the bullet-like confectionary as it came hurtling beyond the stage lights. But these weren't the only dangerous missiles: a large metal pin was thrown on stage at a concert during a summer run in Bournemouth, narrowly missing Paul's eye. With Neil Aspinall's hands now full, another full-time roadie was needed. Malcolm Evans, a former GPO clerk who worked part-time as a bouncer at the Cavern, was hired, having previously driven the group back to Liverpool from London in daunting conditions when Neil was unavailable.

If any one disc could sum up the Beatles' ascent to immortality and evoke what was soon to be defined as Beatlemania it arrived in British record shops on 23rd August, trailed by advance orders of over 300,000. 'She Loves You' refused to budge from the British music-buying public's consciousness throughout the rest of 1963, and Beatle-related news stories would usually incorporate its instantly memorable "Yeah! Yeah! Yeah!" refrain.

In less than a year since the release of 'Love Me Do', the Beatles were in a remarkable position – sell-out concerts, a 15-week BBC series *Pop Go The Beatles* built around them, an official ever-building national fan club, a monthly magazine devoted to their activities and staggering chart statistics. In September they were at the top of the British singles ('She Loves You'), EP (*Twist And Shout*) and LP charts (*Please Please Me*). Already, the EMI pressing plant was bracing itself for the onslaught of advance orders for a second album, which EMI had given the title of *With The Beatles*.

Rattle Your Jewellery

"When we got back to Britain, after we'd
been touring Sweden, this Beatlemania thing
had started, but we didn't hear anything
about it because we'd been away. We just
landed in London and everybody there was
smashing the place up."

George Harrison,
1964 press conference

Friday 13th September
Public Hall, Preston

One of the earliest Beatles concerts covered by the *Daily Mirror*, proving how fan fervour was already rife before Fleet Street gave the name Beatlemania to the phenomenon following the headline-making scenes at the Palladium on 13th October.

The Beatles had spent the previous two days continuing work (which had started in July) on their second album, *With The Beatles*.

Sunday 15th September

Pop Proms, RAH, London

6,000 FANS—THE BEATLES JUST FLED

By DON SHORT

IT was the siege of the Beatle-crushers . . . 6,000 screaming teenagers intent on crushing just four BEATLES.

Never has the Royal Albert Hall seen scenes quite like it. Even for Britain's newly-elected top vocal group, the Beatles it was bewildering. They were appearing at the Great Pop Prom, promoted by Fleetway's top-selling publications — Marilyn, Valentine and Roxy.

In bygone years, litter thrown at an artist was the sign of failure.

Yesterday, when the Beatles—John Lennon, 23; George Harrison, 21; Paul McCartney, 21, and Ringo Starr, 23—came on stage it was the sign of success. They were the target for anything the teenagers could lay their hands on.

Girls swept out of their seats and tried to rush the stage. They were repelled by a solid block of forty commissionaires.

After their final hit number, "Twist and Shout," the four Beatles fled from the stage and out of the Albert Hall into a waiting cab.

Others in the Pop Prom: Shane Fenton, the Brook Brothers, the Fentones, the Lorne Gibson Trio, Arthur Greenslade and the Gee-Men, The Viscounts, the Rolling Stones, Kenny Lynch, Clinton Ford, Susan Maughan and the Vernons Girls.

The show, produced by Donald Maclean and Jimmy Grant, was in aid of the Printers' Pension Corporation.

FATHER SEES BOY PLUNGE TO DEATH

Stephen Evans, 5, slipped, and, as his father watched in horror, fell 150ft. to his death while they were out walking at Symond's Yat, a beauty spot fifteen miles from their Hereford home at the week-end.

At Burnham-on-Sea, Somerset, Hamish Carstairs, 12, of Tingwall Park, Bristol, died when he fell 40ft. down a cliff.

GREVILLE-BELL FREE SOON?

BRITISH businessman Major Anthony Greville-Bell may be freed within the next two days. He signed a petition yesterday for his release from Badajoz jail, Spain, where he has been kept since his arrest on August 29 for alleged smuggling fourteen years ago.

The petition goes today to the Foreign Ministry, which can grant Mr. Greville-Bell his freedom.

The Beatles topped the bill at this afternoon show, promoted by pubescent girl magazines *Valentine*, *Marilyn* and *Roxy* in aid of the Printers' Pension Corporation. The 11 other acts appearing on the bill included the Beatles' closest rivals in the Sixties, the Rolling Stones. The Beatles had met the Stones back in April and became good friends; John and Paul donating 'I Wanna Be Your Man' to the Stones, which they recorded and released as their second single in November, becoming the group's first UK Top 20 hit. On 23rd October the Beatles recorded their own version as a vehicle for Ringo, which completed work on *With The Beatles*.

On 16th September, a relentless schedule of one-nighters around Britain was broken when the Beatles split up to go on holiday; John went to Paris, Paul and Ringo to Athens, sitting in with a local club group the Trio Athenai, while George (and elder brother Peter) went to America to visit their sister Louise in Benton, Illinois. (Louise had emigrated there with her husband in 1956.) Visiting several music stores and clubs, George enquired as to whether they had heard of a group popular in England called the Beatles. He received blank looks.

"I bought a guitar while I was there, a Rickenbacker like John's," George told the *New Musical Express*. "It cost me about £80 or £90 and I had to pay £22 customs' duty on top of that. I didn't get much else except 16 LPs! The Shirelles, the Miracles, Barbara Lewis and so on."

By the time of his return on 3rd October, the momentum surrounding the Beatles continued to build. 'She Loves You' had reached the 750,000 sales mark and continued to climb, earning the group their first gold disc and becoming their first million seller in the UK, while *Please Please Me* had now sold a quarter of a million copies.

Alongside the group's own achievements during that remarkable year of 1963, the success of the Lennon–McCartney song-writing team was further enhanced by the songs knocked off in hotels, coaches and dressing rooms and handed to other artists in Epstein's NEMS management stable – namely Cilla Black (with 'Love Of The Loved'), Tommy Quickly ('Tip Of My Tongue'), the Fourmost ('Hello Little Girl' and 'I'm In Love') and Billy J. Kramer & the Dakotas with no less than five ('Do You Want To Know A Secret', 'I'll Be On My Way', 'Bad To Me', 'I Call Your Name' and 'I'll Keep You Satisfied').

Other artists adapted Beatle songs to their own styles – such as Kenny Lynch with 'Misery' (a song originally intended for Helen Shapiro), Tony Newley and Duffy Power (backed by the Graham Bond Quartet) both covering 'I Saw Her Standing There', the Kestrels re-arrangement of 'There's A Place' and US hitmaker Del Shannon with 'From Me To You', the first American artist to cover a Beatles record.

Sunday 6th October
Carlton Theatre, Kirkcaldy, Scotland

The Beatles' first concert engagements upon their return from holiday were three shows in Scotland, supported by the Caravelles (currently enjoying their one and only hit in 'You Don't Have To Be A Baby To Cry'), the Overlanders (who later had a UK No. 1 in 1966 with their cover of 'Michelle' from *Rubber Soul*), and London outfit Malcolm Clark and the Crestas. The damage caused at the Concert Hall in Glasgow on 5th October put a ban on pop concerts at the venue. George's Rickenbacker (the one he'd bought on his recent American holiday) was nearly stolen from the Beatles' van while in Glasgow but vigilant police recovered it. The following night in Kirkcaldy was less newsworthy, though no less noisy:

*"***Dear Sir** *– Over 2,500 teenagers paid to hear the Beatles at the Carlton Theatre, Kirkcaldy, on Sunday night – myself included. Yet not more than the front three rows in the stalls could possibly have heard them. Starting five minutes before Britain's top pop group took the stage, the screams went on until the curtain came down. I paid to hear the Beatles – not the screams of 1,000 hysterical girls. Deafened, Kirkcaldy."* (Letters page, *Dundee Evening Telegraph and Post*, 8/10/63)

Sunday 13th October
The London Palladium, London

This was the moment when Fleet Street awoke to the phenomenon they memorably labelled 'Beatlemania'. The prestigious event, televised as *Val Parnell's Sunday Night at the London Palladium* and networked live across Britain, was the making of many a star and for the Beatles – Ringo in particular – the Beatles' memorable bill-topping appearance meant that they had truly arrived.

All day, Argyll Street was swamped with nearly 2,000 screaming Beatles' fans battling against a police cordon hoping to catch a glimpse of the group. Inside the theatre the Beatles posed for pictures, including another of the vertically posed "peering round door" shots that photographers seemed to like, and were interviewed in their dressing room for the evening's ITN news.

Reporter: *"Do you deliberately try and create this sort of screaming reaction?"*
Ringo: *"No, we just arrive at the theatre and they're [the fans]*

always there waiting and whenever we're doing a show, the police always come and say 'don't look out the window because you excite them!' (laughter) I'm dying to look out and see them."

The hour-long programme went out at 8.25pm and the Beatles' 12-minute slot consisted of: 'From Me To You', 'I'll Get You', 'She Loves You' and 'Twist And Shout'. The broadcast ended with the Beatles joining the rest of that week's guests on the show's traditional finale, standing on a revolving stage, waving to the audience (and an estimated 15 million TV viewers) to the strains of Jack Parnell's 'Startime'. True showbiz …

Twisting, shouting Beatles fans charge the stage door at the Palladium . . .

Beatles flee in fantastic Palladium TV siege

By MIRROR REPORTER

POLICE fought to hold back more than 1,000 screaming teenagers last night when The Beatles made their "getaway" after their "Sunday Night at the London Palladium" TV performance.

A police motorcycle escort stood by, engines ticking over, as the four pop idols dashed for their car.

Then the fans went wild, breaking through a cordon of more than sixty policemen and stampeding forward.

But The Beatles were just in time.

With engines roaring, their cavalcade raced down Argyle-street and turned into Oxford Circus—heading for a celebration party for the stars' parents and relatives at the Grosvenor House Hotel, Park-lane.

It was the end of a fantastic day-long siege at the Palladium.

At one stage when The Beatles were rehearsing for the A T V show fifty girls managed to break through the emergency doors.

The singers watched as the whooping girls stampeded through the back stalls towards the stage.

Lunch

Stars, attendants and TV technicians tried to block their way. Then somebody threatened to use the fire hose on them.

The manager, Mr. David Wilmot, dialled 999. And as the police ran into the theatre the girls ran out.

The top-of-the-bill Beatles —John Lennon, Paul McCartney, George Harrison and Ringo Starr—were forbidden to leave the Palladium.

Said John: "We were going out for lunch. Instead we had roast lamb, potatoes and sprouts served in our dressing rooms."

Later the Beatles, who all come from Liverpool, told Palladium chief Val Parnell that they wanted a stroll before the performance.

He said: " I am not risk-

MOTOR-CYCLE GUARD GETS THEM AWAY

ing letting you out. It could be dangerous."

So they popped their heads round the stage door to have a look at the fans massed outside.

There was a tremendous screech — and the girls flung themselves at the gate just in front of them.

Inside the theatre hundreds of fans made the show the noisiest in the history of "Sunday Night."

Clothes

The teenagers—many of the boys dressed in high-necked tight-fitting Beatles type clothes—screamed and shouted for the pop group.

"You could do nothing with them—they were just mad for the Beatles," said comedian Des O'Connor who appeared on the Palladium programme immediately before the Liverpool lads.

After the show the crowds outside prevented other stars from leaving.

The Beatles (from the top) Paul, John, George and Ringo, at the Palladium yesterday.

Today's weather

Sunny spells at first, cloudy later. Warmer. OUTLOOK: Cloudy, rain in places, bright spells.

London area, S.E., Central-Southern England, E. Anglia, E. Midlands, Channel Islands: Sunny periods, becoming cloudy in evening but probably dry. Max. temp. 17C (63F).

S.W. England, S. Wales and Mon.: Sunny periods, cloudy in afternoon. Per-

haps rain in evening. Max. temp. 16C (61F).

E. England, W. Midlands: Sunny periods, cloudy in evening. Max. temp. 16C (61F).

SUNSET: Birmingham, 6.17; Bristol, 6.22; Derby, 6.17; Plymouth, 6.29; London, 6.12.

A ROYAL SHOW FOR THE BEATLES

By DON SHORT

GIRLS fight police to get at them. Fervid fans queue hours to see them. But yesterday The Beatles won their greatest honour.

They were invited to join the stars in the Royal Variety Show at London's Prince of Wales theatre on November 4.

And the four lads who have sent the Liverpool Sound pounding through a million transistor sets can thank a 16-year-old art student.

She is Susan Delfont.

Her father, impresario Bernard Delfont, is the man who picked the stars to perform before the Queen Mother—and possibly Princess Margaret.

He said last night : " I didn't know who The Beatles were until five months ago.

Record

" Susan asked me for an extra ten bob pocket money to buy one of their records.

" I had to ask her: 'Who are The Beatles?' I told her not to worry about the cash as I could get the record, 'Please, please me.' at wholesale price.

" But she was so insistent about it that when I got to

And Marlene will star

work I sent my secretary out to buy it.

It has taken The Beatles just two years to rise from the obscurity of a basement coffee-bar—where they performed as The Quarrymen for £7 10s. a night—to the dizzy heights of a Command Performance.

With them on the bill is Marlene Dietrich—at fifty-eight, still the world's most glamorous grandma.

And for a style contrast there is the pop girl the boys boosted into the Top Ten—Susan Maughan.

Max Bygraves will be making his eleventh royal appearance. Dickie Henderson, Harry Secombe,

Tommy Steele and Charlie Drake are also old hands.

There is no male pop solo singer in the show.

Also left out is Sammy Davis, Junior—though it is only a month ago since he said he would definitely be taking part.

A Delfont spokesman said last night that "he overlooked the fact that he could not possibly come because of a film contract."

From television there is the " Steptoe and Son" team of Wilfrid Brambell and Harry H. Corbett.

And, after 34 years as a top bandleader, Joe Loss gets recognition, too.

The Queen will not see the show. She is expecting her fourth baby.

NOW IT'S THE BIG TIME

AND this is yesterday's picture of The Beatles. Now they are in the Big Time Nowadays, John, Ringo, Paul and George (from the left) mix with the stars. And the man in front? That's The Beatles' oldest fan—they call him " Uncle Paddy".

As a mob waited at the stage door on Great Marlborough Street, Neil Aspinall arranged for the Beatles to emerge from the front of the theatre where he drove them away from the reach of frantic fans who discovered the ruse. Afterwards, the Beatles went on to a party thrown by Brian Epstein for family and friends at the Grosvenor House Hotel. While the sound balance on the Beatles' segment fell short of their standards, the critical reception was a general thumbs up.

The next day's tabloids brought this new showbiz happening onto their front pages, a position it rarely left for the next two years.

October continued to be an eventful month. On the 15th, it was announced that the Beatles had been invited by Bernard Delfont to appear in the annual Royal Variety Performance at London's Prince of Wales Theatre on 4th November.

ITN reporter: "Paul, have you thought about your act for the show yet? Any changes in the act or is it going to be the usual routine?"

Paul: "No, we'll have to change it, I'm sure, but we can't do the same thing all the time. We haven't thought about what we're going to do yet."

Reporter: "Suits with collars on, brushed, parted hair, something like that?"

Paul: "You never know, we might not wear suits!"

Reporter: "John, in this Royal Variety Show when you'll be appearing before royalty, your language has got to be pretty good

"GAD, SMITHERS, WHAT NEXT?"

obviously, what about this thing in the news about Ted Heath saying he couldn't distinguish you speaking the Queen's English."
John: *(affecting posh voice)* *"I can't understand Teddy saying that at all, really. (To camera) We're not going to vote for Ted!"*

The Beatles were back at EMI Studios two days later to record both sides of their fifth single, 'I Want To Hold Your Hand' and 'This Boy', as well as recording the first of an annual fixture – the Beatles' own Christmas recording pressed on a flexi disc and given away to members of the Official Beatles Fan Club. (This practice continued each year up to the Beatles' dissolution in 1969.) Said Paul: "We just felt we'd been really lucky over the year and we wanted to think of a way of saying thank you." Not released until 29th November, 'I Want To Hold Your Hand' already attracted advance sales of 500,000.

Saturday 19th October
Pavilion Gardens Ballroom, Buxton

2

The last ballroom date the Beatles ever played. The sheer dangers involved – as witnessed by the crush evident in these pictures – was the deciding factor. Also, the Beatles' sheer popularity made the economics impractical. From now on, the Beatles would only play theatre dates in their homeland.

On 31st October the Beatles arrived back from Sweden where they had spent the past week on their first foreign tour, recording for radio and TV as well as playing nine concerts around the country; the Swedes had soon fallen into line.

The welcoming committee of 1,500 screaming fans was

memorable for several reasons, and was the first of the typical airport welcomes the Beatles would receive, either departing for or returning from a foreign foray. Sir Alec Douglas-Home, flying to Edinburgh on his way back to his election campaign, and the pulchritudinous contestants arriving for the Miss World contest went virtually unnoticed, as did top-rated American television host Ed Sullivan who, by sheer (and lucky) coincidence, happened to be delayed at London Airport.

Wondering what all the commotion was about and having never heard of these Beatles, Sullivan nevertheless recognized they merited further investigation and got his scout to contact Brian Epstein to arrange for them to appear on his popular Sunday night coast-to-coast variety show in New York. Sullivan wanted the group as guest stars, but Epstein insisted on top billing. He got his way and a contract was agreed on Monday 11th November.

The Beatles' car arrives at the Odeon, Winchcombe Street, Cheltenham.

Friday 1st November
Odeon Cinema, Cheltenham

The opening night of the Beatles' five-week, sell-out UK tour, for which they commanded a nightly fee of £300. At most of the shows, the *Daily Mirror's* local "stringer" was on hand to cover events as was a photographer, which proved that the usual Beatlemania symptoms – screaming, fainting, delirium – were well in evidence even in this most genteel of English spa towns. Getting the Beatles in and out of theatres was planned like a military manoeuvre involving police liaising with theatre managers and the Beatles' representatives outside the towns and cities visited. *Record Mirror* reported that support act Peter Jay and the Jaywalkers were so worried about touring with the Beatles that they had insured themselves for £35,000.

1. THE RHYTHM & BLUES QUARTET
2. Frank Berry introduces THE VERNONS GIRLS
3. FRANK BERRY
4. THE BROOK BROTHERS
5. FRANK BERRY
6. PETER JAY & THE JAYWALKERS

interval

7. THE RHYTHM & BLUES QUARTET
8. THE KESTRELS
9. FRANK BERRY
10. **THE BEATLES**

In accordance with the requirements of the Watch Committee (a) The Public may leave at the end of the performance by all exit and entrance doors and such doors must, at that time be open (b) All gangways, passage and staircases must be kept entirely free from chairs or other obstructions (c) Persons shall not be permitted to stand or sit in any of the intersecting gangways or stand in any unseated space in the Auditorium, unless standing in such space has been specially allowed by the Watch Committee. Notice is exhibited in that part of the Auditorium in which standing has been sanctioned. (d) The safety curtain must be lowered and raised in the presence of each audience, where applicable. PROGRAMME SUBJECT TO ALTERATION

Set-list for the tour: *'I Saw Her Standing There', 'From Me To You', 'All My Loving', 'You Really Got A Hold On Me', 'Roll Over Beethoven', 'Boys', 'Till There Was You', 'She Loves You', 'Money' and 'Twist And Shout' (with a brief instrumental burst of 'From Me To You' as the curtain closed).*

Saturday 2nd November
City Hall, Sheffield

The Beatles' first northern tour date: and, as if they didn't already have enough to cope with, Sheffield University students had planned to kidnap the Beatles upon their arrival as a Rag Day stunt. A spokesman for the Rag Committee told Sheffield paper *The Star*: "We wrote to the Beatles to ask them if they would co-operate in the plot. We had an extremely nice letter in reply from the group, saying it would all be good for a laugh, but, what with it being Rag Day and the day of their show in the city, they thought the idea might be a bit foolhardy because of the possible reaction of their fans."

"Beatles Keep It A Secret": *"Secret plans have been drawn up by the Beatles for their visit to Sheffield tonight. At their London headquarters a rota of arrival times and hotel bookings has been drafted – and put under lock and key,"* said the group's press officer, Mr Tony Barrow, last night: *"The plans are top secret – we daren't even tell the Press about them. The sight of a couple of photographers would have crowds there by the hundreds in a matter of minutes."* (Sheffield Telegraph, 2/11/63)

Sunday 3rd November
Odeon Cinema, Leeds

A bomb scare was reported but police correctly treated it as a hoax, averting a potentially horrific stampede by 2,500 fans toward the exits.

"*Beatlemania such as was seen in Leeds during the weekend and no doubt will be seen in London tonight at the Command Performance, is not a problem intentionally created by the four young fellows. The screaming mania among little girls is the problem. Why do they do it? Ask one of the squealers and she will probably be unable to explain beyond saying in all seriousness, 'I just think they're fab.'*" (*Yorkshire Evening Post editorial*, 4/11/63)

"*An ardent admirer of the Beatles, I looked forward for weeks to seeing them in Leeds and that is about all that happened – I SAW them. The audience screamed the compere off the stage when he appealed for quietness. Throughout the Beatles' performance, hardly a word could be heard. Even when the boys themselves asked the audience in no uncertain terms to shut up, there was no response, although obviously the Beatles were getting most annoyed.*" (Letter to *Yorkshire Evening Post*, 6/11/63)

The Beatles dash into the Prince of Wales Theatre, Coventry Street, London and (below) greeting dignitaries.

Monday 4th November
Royal Variety Show, Prince of Wales Theatre, London

The Beatles made their memorable "jewel-rattling" appearance before the Queen Mother and Princess Margaret and Lord Snowdon. Also appearing for the first time at this annual show biz fixture were Susan Maughan, Marlene Dietrich, and Buddy Greco. Previous participants returning to the top prestige event were Max Bygraves, Tommy Steele (joined by the cast of *Half A Sixpence*), Dickie Henderson, Charlie Drake and Harry Secombe (with the *Pickwick* company).

Other artists taking part on an eclectic bill included Joe Loss and his orchestra, Wilfred Brambell and Harry H. Corbett (*Steptoe And Son*), Michael Flanders and Donald Swann, Eric Sykes and Hattie Jacques, Pinky and Perky, and Los Paraguayos. A total of £32,500 was paid by ATV and the BBC for the respective television and broadcasting rights.

"A 60-strong police squad – treble the usual size – has been detailed for duty for tonight's Royal Variety Performance before the Queen Mother in case Beatle fans give trouble. The strictest precautions have been devised to protect the Queen Mother when she arrives at

the Prince of Wales Theatre shortly before 8.30pm. Rehearsals for the show went on until midnight last night and they were under way again by mid-morning today. The Beatles, fingers protecting their ears, burst into the theatre today [at 11am] inches ahead of 200 screaming teenage fans."(Birmingham Evening Mail and Despatch, 4/11/63)

Rehearsing for the Royal Variety Show.

Royal Performance in the presence of Her Majesty The Queen Mother on the Evening of Monday November 4th 1963 at The Prince of Wales Theatre, London.

THE BEATLES BY ROYAL COMMAND

"Earlier yesterday about 300 teenagers collected outside the theatre hoping to see the Beatles leave after morning rehearsals. But they were disappointed, because the group left by a rear exit to go to a nearby restaurant for lunch." (Daily Mirror, 5/11/63)

Dressed in their new black suits, as the curtain opened on the Beatles' spot, the group went into 'From Me To You' followed by 'She Loves You'. Paul then nervously introduced 'Till There Was You' as being by "our favourite American group, Sophie Tucker". John then announced the last number, 'Twist And Shout' by asking, "would the people in the cheaper seats, clap your hands. And if the rest of you, if you'd just rattle your jewellery." With the last notes of 'Twist And Shout', the Beatles grouped at the front of the stage, turned and bowed low to the Royal Box and then turned and raced off stage left. No encores were allowed, so compere Dickie Henderson waited for the enthusiastic applause to die down before quipping, "The Beatles… young… talented… frightening!"

If there were any sceptics still unsure as to the Beatles' appeal this was surely the moment their cynicism melted. The Beatles and Lennon's quip were all over the next day's dailies and the group were suddenly being appreciated by the older generation as well.

The old showbiz establishment of Harry Secombe, Tommy Steele and Marlene Dietrich meet the new stars.

The Beatles did not emerge from the Prince of Wales until 1.30am, by which time police outnumbered the fans who had remained to see them leave an after-show party.

Wednesday 6th November
ABC Cinema, Northampton

"Beatles 'Escape' In National Anthem"
"It all went off without a hitch, a Northampton Borough police spokesman said today. While the crowds were milling around outside, the Beatles were already on their way to London down the M1.

They were smuggled out while the National Anthem was being played. This was the carefully thought out 'escape' plan used by the police as crowds of chanting Beatles fans collected in Abington Square and at the two exits from the ABC car park a coach charged out of the Lower Mount exit and dashed away.
Inside were most of the supporting acts – but not the Beatles. While this decoy was being mobbed by the fans, the four Liverpudlians were making their way under police escort across the car park at the rear of the cinema and through a factory into St Michaels's Road where a car sped them away to safety." (Northampton Chronicle and Echo, 7/11/63).

Friday 8th November
Ritz Cinema, Belfast

2

The Beatles had flown into Dublin the previous day, playing two shows at the city's Adelphi Theatre. George also caught up with some of his Irish cousins. Accompanying the group was Liverpool playright Alun Owen, who had been engaged to write the screenplay for the Beatles' first film for United Artists, which was to start shooting the following March. (The Beatles, and Paul McCartney in particular, were fans of Owen's 1959 play *No Trams To Lime Street*.) Owen's screenplay almost wrote itself as he saw how the Beatles' fame confined them to hotel rooms and backstage dressing rooms.

On the 8th the Beatles left Dublin at 11.45am, driving over the border on the Dundalk to Newry Road. Before the first show the Beatles met the press at the Ritz Cinema, as well as 17-year-old Audrey Gowar, secretary of the Irish Beatles Fan Club. The original plan was to have support act Peter Jay and the Jaywalkers create a diversion by arriving at the front while the Beatles sneaked around the back, disguised under flat caps. However, the commissioner of the Royal Ulster Constabulary insisted: "The Beatles must be seen, otherwise there will be riots." The group's entrance to the cinema involved 300 policemen forcing a passage through the crowds gathered outside.

John films the other Beatles in the stalls of the Belfast Ritz. Where is that cine film now?

Arriving back from Belfast with roadie Mal Evans (behind).
Overleaf: On stage at Granada, East Ham.

Saturday 9th November
Granada Cinema, East Ham

The Beatles almost missed the plane from Belfast for London. They slept in at the Grand Central Hotel and made a mad dash to Aldegrove Airport. That evening, George Martin visited the group in their dressing room in East London to announce almost a 1 million advance sales figure for 'I Want To Hold Your Hand'.

Sunday 10th November

Hippodrome Theatre, Birmingham

The Beatles were smuggled into the theatre yard in a Black Maria, thinly disguised wearing police helmets – a publicity stunt on the authorities' part rather than a security measure. On their way up from London the group's black Austin

Roadie Mal Evans is swamped as he loads the Beatles' gear into the Birmingham Hippodrome.

Princess broke down on the M1 and was towed off by an RAC vehicle. While the car was repaired the group had a meal then drove as arranged, but later than expected, direct to the Birmingham police headquarters on Steelhouse Lane. "The police were very cooperative," said George. "They gave us a cup of tea and we gave them our autographs. We left our own car there and rode to the theatre in a Black Maria with seven policemen after putting on the police helmets and mackintoshes."

"Bawl beats the Beatles"
"They screamed and they shrieked and they stamped their feet. Whatever the decibel rating (and it must have been shattering), the audience were the ear-piercing victors when the Beatles appeared here last night... Entertainment? It all depends, of course, how you interpret it. But if the audience beat the Beatles with the sound barrier, the Merseysiders had the best view of the amazing spectacle. After all, they were four young men who were being paid handsomely to entertain two capacity audiences of 2,000 at each show, and they were able to watch the strange antics of the 4,000 who paid to see them. It was quite impossible to hear any announcement made by the group. On occasions, there was an appeal for silence, but the reaction was an even greater explosion of audience sound, hysterics and demonstrations. The stage was bombarded with far more than noise. Teddy bears, boxes of chocolates, photographs, programmes and sundry missiles were aimed at the performers. Then, with a sudden, stunning emphasis, down came the curtain – and the safety curtain. It was all over. By the time the National Anthem had been played the Beatles were out of the theatre and driving away from Birmingham. And within 10 minutes, the theatre that had rocked with noise was uncannily silent – and empty." (Excerpt from Birmingham Evening Mail and Despatch review, 11/11/63)

SUNDAY NOV. 10TH
THE BEATLES
ALL SEATS & STANDING ROOM COMPLETELY
SOLD OUT

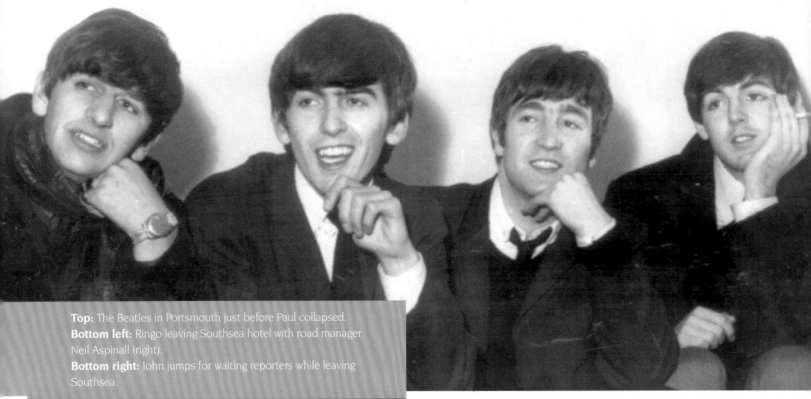

Top: The Beatles in Portsmouth just before Paul collapsed.
Bottom left: Ringo leaving Southsea hotel with road manager Neil Aspinall (right).
Bottom right: John jumps for waiting reporters while leaving Southsea.

Tuesday 12th November

The only occasion when a British Beatles show had to be cancelled and re-arranged occurred when the group reached the south coast city of Portsmouth. Both George and Paul had caught flu but Paul's case of gastric flu was more serious. An appearance for Southern Television in neighbouring Southampton was cancelled, and after weakly meeting the press backstage at the Guildhall, Paul was sent to bed with a high temperature while promoter Arthur Howes was forced to cancel the evening shows at the last minute – news of which made national headlines. The shows were rescheduled to Tuesday 3rd December.

Driver Bill Corbett pilots the Beatles' Austin Princess away to Plymouth.

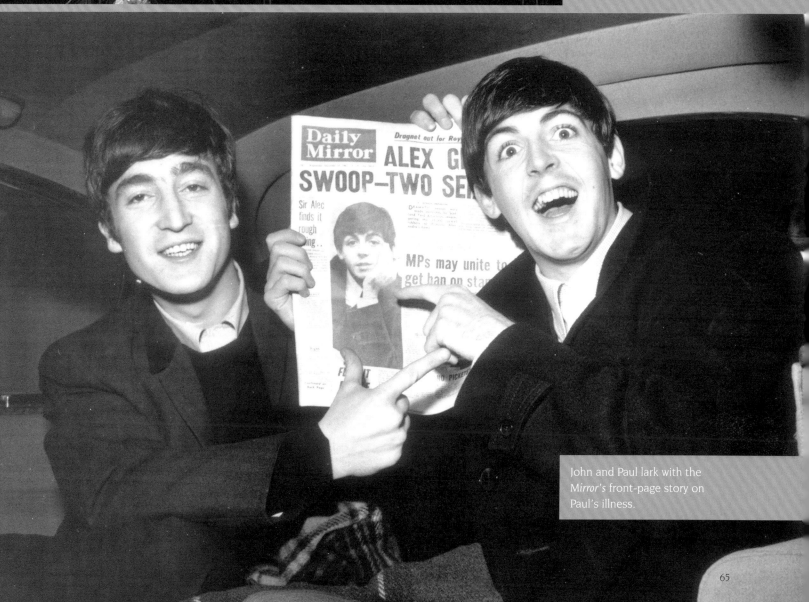

John and Paul lark with the *Mirror's* front-page story on Paul's illness.

Wednesday 13th November 2
ABC Cinema, Plymouth

Since the phone didn't stop ringing at the ABC, Arthur Howes released a press statement to assure fans that the night's two shows in Plymouth were going ahead. With Paul (and George)

being examined by a doctor and given flu jabs at the Royal Beach Hotel, Southsea, the Beatles set out in high spirits on the 165-mile drive. A smiling Paul, feigning collapsing ill to waiting press, said, "I'm much better".

Before the concert the Beatles appeared being interviewed at the studios of Westward Television in Plymouth. The group walked from the studio back to the ABC Theatre via a tunnel connecting the neighbouring buildings on Derry's Cross.

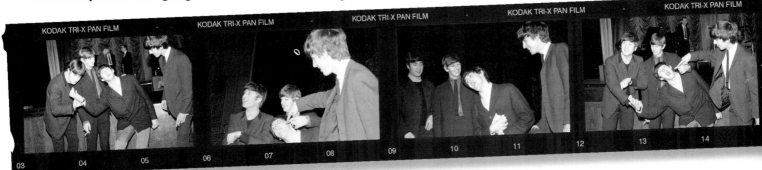

Paul and George on stage in Plymouth and the heavily guarded dash for the car from the ABC stage door.

Thursday 14th November
ABC Cinema, Exeter

When the Beatles weren't being cornered by press and photographers backstage, to kill the hours before showtime, they would sometimes join in casual jam sessions with some of the support groups on the tour.

Thursday 14th and Sunday 17th November

Beatles' queues in Lewisham, south London and Southend-on-Sea, Essex.

These pictures are indicative of the type of incredible scenes of Beatles ticket queues around Britain. Up to 48 hours before the box offices were to open, fans would camp out through the night to ensure getting the best seats. (The Lewisham queue – for two shows on Sunday 8 December – started on Thursday night, with police costs estimated at over £400, while in Southend (for shows on 9 December), the cost of controlling the queue was a staggering £1,200.

With extra security laid on the Beatles were called upon to account as to whether this was what taxpayers money should be spent on. "Look we don't ask for it all," Paul told the press. "If the authorities think it is safer to lay on extra police, you can't blame us. We just don't want anybody to get hurt, especially the fans."

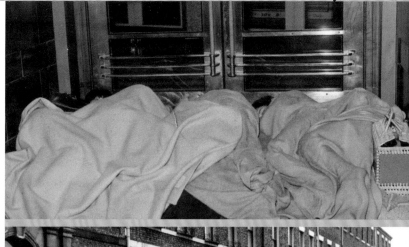

The Beatles meet their public backstage in Coventry and (right) teach actress Julie Christie a new chord.

Queues for this show started minutes after the Beatles' Palladium television appearance on 13th October. By the morning, hours before the box office opened, the queue had grown to 2,000 and theatre officials described it as "fantastic".

Backstage the Beatles indulged in their latest hobby to keep them occupied; Scalextric racing cars on 30 feet of track set up in the backstage bar. "It's good fun and helps keep us relaxed," Ringo told the *Mirror*.

"Last night, over 4,000 fans attended two performances at the Coventry Theatre… Ear-splitting roars greeted the Beatles' appearances on stage and they were showered with tokens of affection including dolls, flowers and jelly babies. Several girls were overcome with hysterics, and smelling salts were used to revive them. Outside the theatre there were also scenes of excitement as fans who had braved the rain waited hopefully for a glimpse of their idols. They kept up chants of 'It's the Beatles' during the two shows." (*Coventry Evening Telegraph*, 18/11/63)

Off the Beatle track in Coventry.

Thursday 21st November
ABC Cinema, Carlisle

Showing they weren't ones to hold grudges, the Beatles stayed at the Crown and Mitre Hotel where, almost nine months earlier as support act on the Helen Shapiro tour, they had been ejected from the ballroom as uninvited guests by Bill Berry, chairman of the Carlisle Golf Club, during the club's annual dinner-dance, for wearing leather jackets.

The same day Beatlemania hit Cumbria the group made news when being mentioned in the House of Commons for the first time. MP Sir Charles Taylor (Eastbourne, C) questioned the financial cost of police protection for the Beatles.

John Lennon: "Somebody told me he'd had a nervous breakdown, the fella who's complaining. I don't know if it's true but I heard he was a bit funny."

Friday 22nd November
Globe Cinema, Stockton-on-Tees

2

An eventful day in more ways than one – as well as being the official release date for the group's second LP, *With The Beatles*, Teeside fans leaving the early 6:15pm show were stunned to hear the news of President John F. Kennedy's assassination in Dallas, Texas (the news came through to the UK about 7pm).

After the 8:30pm show in Stockton, the Beatles were whisked off in a car to a secret hideout "somewhere in the north east", according to the *Evening Chronicle*.

Friday 29th November
ABC Cinema, Huddersfield

On this day 'I Want To Hold Your Hand' was released, and the following week the Beatles earned their second gold disc for a million sold in the UK. It also knocked their first million seller and current No. 1, 'She Loves You', down to No. 2. The British pop business had never seen the like of it before.

Ringo checks out support act Peter Jay's drum kit backstage at Huddersfield.

Wednesday 11th December
Futurist Theatre, Scarborough

"It is now three days since Scarborough was bombarded by the Beatles – but the memory lingers on, and they remain the talking point for most of the teenagers and their families. Their one-night appearance on the Scarborough scene has had a tremendous effect on everything connected with them. Three shops report that their record sales have shot up since Thursday morning. 'We had a terrific demand for their records before they came, and now we are selling the discs as fast as we can get them,' said a spokesman at one. Another shop reported buyers as 'coming in droves', and the third shop reported 'fantastic' sales." (Scarborough Evening News, 14/12/63)

————— THE BEATLES' FAN CLUB —————

PRIORITY OPPORTUNITY TO PURCHASE BY POST THE FIRST 1,000 TICKETS FOR A

Grand   Public   Dance

starring

THE BEATLES

at

Wimbledon   Palais   Ballroom

**SATURDAY
14 DECEMBER**

TICKETS
IN
ADVANCE **10/- EACH**

EVENING   DANCE   BEGINS   AT 7·30 p.m.

MEMBERS OF THE OFFICIAL BEATLES FAN CLUB HAVE A SPECIAL OPPORTUNITY OF PURCHASING TICKETS IN ADVANCE BY POST FOR THIS PUBLIC DANCE. ONLY ONE THOUSAND TICKETS ARE BEING RESERVED FOR FAN CLUB USE. THEREFORE MEMBERS WHO WISH TO ATTEND ARE URGED TO COMPLETE AND RETURN THE FORM BELOW AS SOON AS POSSIBLE. TICKETS ARE TEN SHILLINGS EACH AND THE FAN CLUB WILL PAY THE COST OF POSTING TICKETS TO MEMBERS.

YOUR ORDER FORM MAY BE ENCLOSED WITH YOUR APPLICATION TO ATTEND THE FAN CLUB GET-TOGETHER BUT PLEASE MAKE SURE THAT YOU ATTACH A POSTAL ORDER COVERING THE COST OF TICKETS (AT 10/- EACH) YOU ARE ORDERING FOR THE PUBLIC DANCE.

Saturday 14th December
Palais, Wimbledon, London

As the Beatles had held a special Northern Area Fan Club get together in Liverpool the previous weekend (on Saturday 7th December at the Liverpool Empire, which was filmed by the BBC and broadcast later that evening as *It's The Beatles*) the Southern Area Fan Club Convention was held in the afternoon at this since-bulldozed ballroom. As well as performing, the Beatles sat behind the bar from 1.30-4pm to meet some of the 3,000 fans who had queued for hours over the Palais dance floor – shaking hands and (for a time) signing autographs as the large procession filed past. The group then performed their usual concert repertoire (see 1st November for details).

Not wishing for their precious stage to be defiled, the venue's management erected a temporary platform for the group to perform on. Despite over 100 police on duty the Beatles were displeased to see the fans cooped up behind a makeshift wire cage, prompting John Lennon's infamous quip, "If they press any harder [against the fence], they'll come through as chips!"

Saturday 21st December
Gaumont Cinema, Bradford

Despite thick fog and heavy rain, a queue of 2,000 fans had waited up to 12 hours for tickets to this preview of the Beatles' Christmas Show, attended by 3,000 at each house. The sketches and sets to be featured in the London stage show were left out, the Beatles (and the other acts on the bill) performing only their musical segments.

The Beatles set (as also performed in London): 'Roll Over Beethoven', 'All My Loving', 'This Boy', 'I Wanna Be Your Man', 'She Loves You', 'Till There Was You', 'I Want To Hold Your Hand', 'Money' and 'Twist And Shout'.

Afterwards Mrs Mavis Wood, Lady Mayoress of Bradford, commented, "The Beatles were good, but what a noise!" Jimmy Savile was in the audience and the Beatles acknowledged the DJ by dedicating 'Money' to him.

The Beatles had arrived in Bradford from London at about 4pm and watched their pre-taped appearance on the 'Lucky Stars On Merseyside' edition of the weekly Saturday evening pop programme *Thank Your Lucky Stars* in their dressing room. The following night the Xmas preview played the Liverpool Empire before opening in London on the 24th.

The Beatles with Christmas Show cast pictured onstage at the Finsbury Park Astoria, London.

Tuesday 24th December – Tuesday 31st December

"The Beatles' Christmas Show", Astoria Cinema, Finsbury Park, London

Produced by Peter Yolland, Brian Epstein had arranged this season of family-oriented shows back in October. All 100,000 tickets had sold-out within 25 days of going on sale with the by now customary overnight queues to get the best seats.

After the curtain rose, the Beatles were first seen jumping out of a giant Christmas cracker and then descending from a cardboard helicopter (The S.S Beatle) on to the stage as compere Rolf Harris introduced each performer on the bill to take their bow. The Beatles popped up in further skits between the acts (appearing, in order) the Barron Knights and Duke D'Mond, Tommy Quickly (backed by the Barron Knights), the Fourmost, and Billy J. Kramer and the Dakotas (closing the first half) with the second half featuring the Barron Knights who also backed Cilla Black, while the unenviable slot before the Beatles was admirably filled by Rolf Harris.

For the pantomime in the first half, entitled 'What A Night' in which Fearless Paul the Signalman rescued Ermyntrude Our Heroine (George) from the villainous Sir John Jasper (John) off the railway track, while Ringo ran across the stage sprinkling paper snow, the Beatles often mimed to a pre-recorded tape over the antiquated PA system as the fans made the group's own voices inaudible. The dialogue was also presented on a screen behind them as they spoke.

After the opening shows on Xmas Eve, Brian Epstein arranged a special chartered flight to take the Beatles and most of the cast back to Liverpool to spend Christmas with their families, returning to London on Boxing Day morning.

At the year's end 'I Want To Hold Your Hand' and 'She Loves You' were at numbers one and two respectively, With The Beatles and Please Please Me were occupying the two top positions on the LP charts, and Twist And Shout, The Beatles No. 1 and The Beatles Hits filled the top three slots in the EP charts. The Beatles had notched up total record sales of over 4 million copies in less than 12 months. 30,000 paid up members belonged to the Official Beatles Fan Club.

Without doubt, the Beatles had totally revitalized a moribund British pop scene. And to think, only a year before, they were practically unknown outside Liverpool.

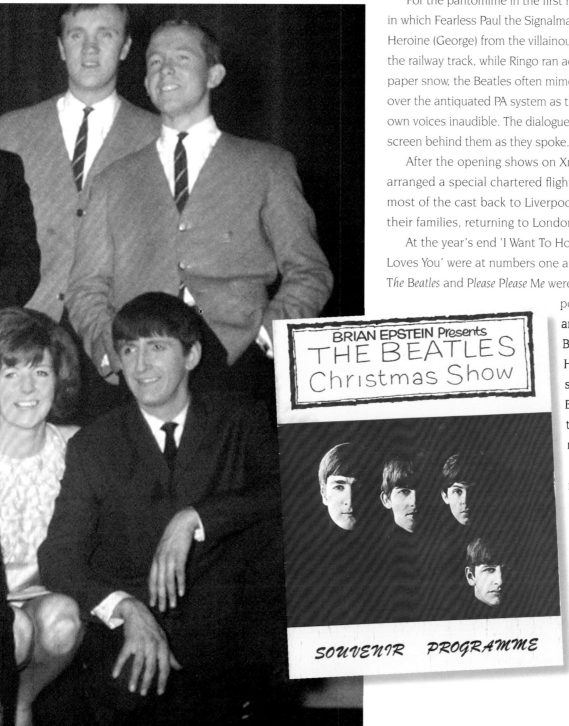

BRIAN EPSTEIN Presents
THE BEATLES Christmas Show

SOUVENIR PROGRAMME

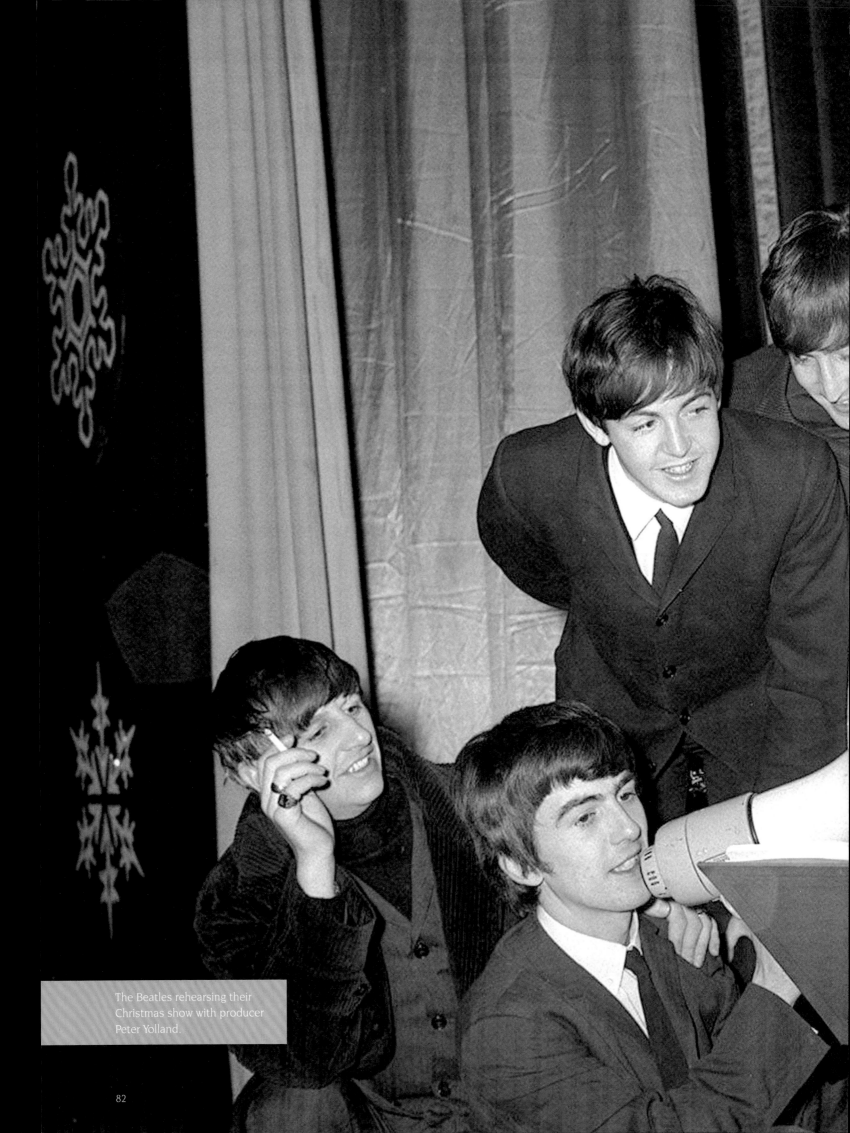

The Beatles rehearsing their
Christmas show with producer
Peter Yolland.

A Hard Day's Night In America

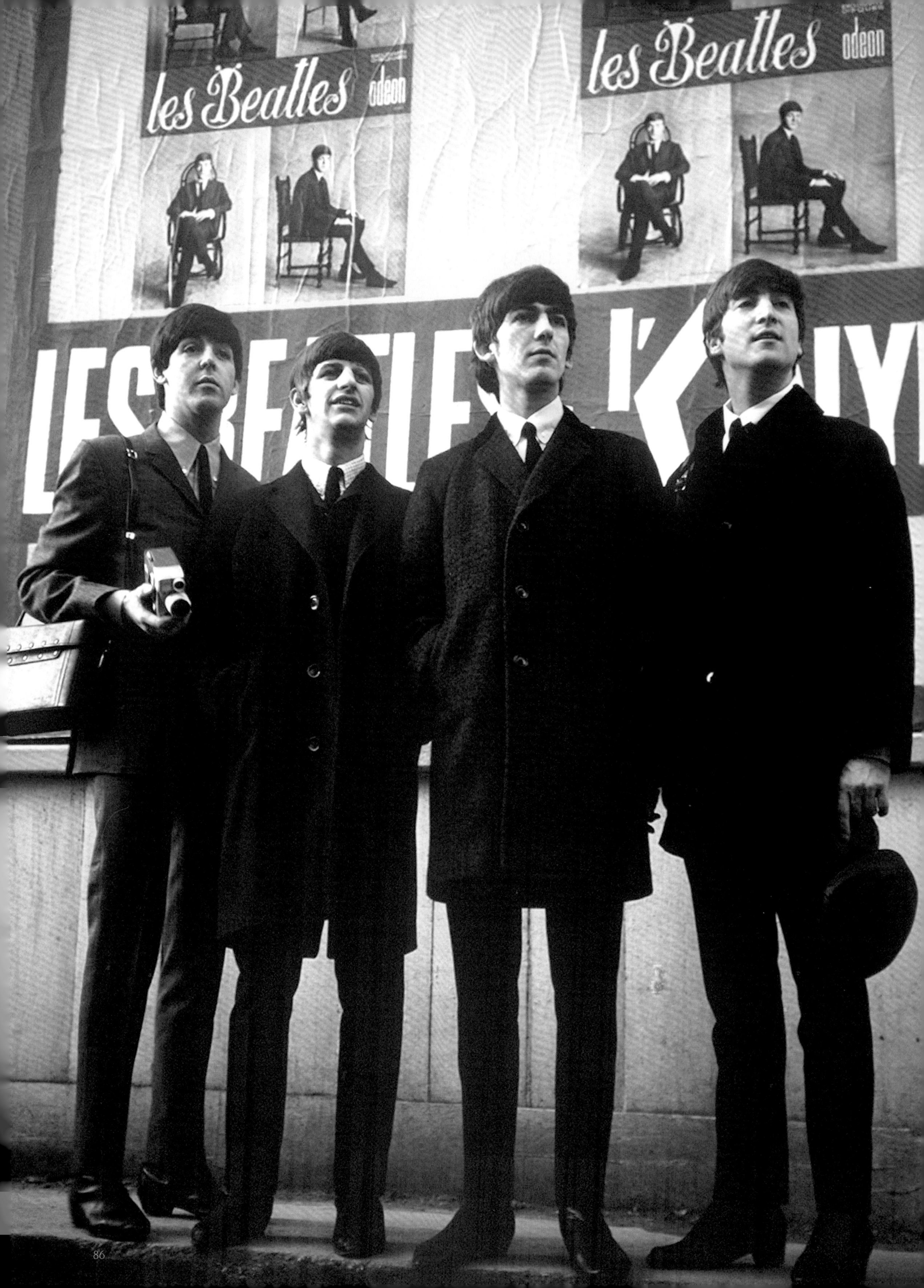
les Beatles
odeon
les Beatles
odeon

At the start of the year Beatlemania in Britain showed no signs of abatement, with 'I Want To Hold Your Hand' eclipsing the sales of 'She Loves You', selling over one and a half million copies. Beatles records were also selling fast throughout Europe and such far-flung territories as Australia, New Zealand, South Africa, Japan and the Philippines. In January, the group undertook a season at the Paris Olympia (a booking made by Brian Epstein the previous July) where the cool Parisian audiences – mostly male – either clapped or roared their approval, which the Beatles initially found disorientating considering they had spent the best part of the last six months drowned out by shrill female screams. However, 1964 will forever be associated as the year that American resistance to the Beatles broke down in a wholly unprecedented fashion.

From inauspicious beginnings – the Beatles recordings had been released on a string of small independent US labels, namely Vee Jay, based in Chicago, and Swan out of Philadelphia – the staggering British sales of 'She Loves You' and, in particular, 'I Want To Hold Your Hand' made Capitol, EMI's American subsidiary, finally sit up and take notice. With 'I Want To Hold Your Hand' being rush-released in late December (Billboard picked the single as its "Spotlight Winner Of The Week", while fellow industry journal Cash Box made it "Pick Of The Week" describing the record as "an infectious twist-like thumper that could spread like wildfire here"), in January, the label invested an impressive $50,000 into a massive publicity campaign that ensured the word Beatles would no longer bring to mind images of the creepy-crawly bug.

Within 10 days of its US issue 'I Want To Hold Your Hand' had sold almost half a million copies, entering the Billboard chart at 45, while soaring from its initial Cash Box entry at 80 to 43, making it the fastest-selling ever British disc in America to date. Previously, the Americans had only made successes of a few British releases by the likes of Acker Bilk, Kenny Ball, Rolf Harris and Frank Ifield.

The American media seemed to be obsessed by the Beatles' "cereal bowl haircuts" and whether they really were wearing wigs. "The Beatles are part of a strong-flowing reaction against the soft, middle-class south of England, which has controlled popular culture for so long," wrote the New York Times Sunday Magazine supplement. "The most popular thing about the Beatles is that they come from Liverpool."

As an indication of how far the Americans capitulated, in the first week of April, the Beatles hogged the first five places on the national Billboard 'Hot 100', with seven other Beatles singles showing within the countdown – an amazing accomplishment and one that has never been equalled by any other artist. The Beatles' astounding breakthrough in the United States opened the floodgates to a wide array of British groups and singers that subsequently came to be dubbed "The British Invasion".

Following the group's successful visit to the States in February, they embarked on a dizzying schedule: recording sessions, making their first, critically acclaimed film A Hard Day's Night in just eight weeks, as well as various radio and TV appearances and an hour-long special, Around The Beatles. In the middle of this, John's first book of nonsense verse, In His Own Write, was published. All of these small-screen appearances were mimed to please the television companies who preferred this so as to make their sound problems easier. (The Beatles didn't make a truly live television musical appearance in Britain in 1964 apart from a return to Sunday Night At the London Palladium on 12th January, and Mike and Bernie Winters' summer spectacular Blackpool Night Out on 19th July.)

Your Invitation to the PRESS SHOW of "A HARD DAY'S NIGHT"

released on 27th November to advance orders of over 750,000 and the group's seventh consecutive No. 1 single in Britain.

By the end of the year, in typical tall poppy fashion, the British press started speculating that Beatlemania had lost its intensity. During October no less an authority than the Duke of Edinburgh, Prince Philip, supposedly remarked to a folk group, the Travellers, while on a royal visit to Canada that, "Now's the time to come to England – the Beatles are on the wane." When his comments made headlines he ordered an instant retraction, sending a cable to the Beatles' office, which read:

"Disregard press reports quoting the Duke of Edinburgh as saying Beatles on the wane. Should read: 'I think the Beatles are away at the moment.' Mistake probably due to misprint. Prince Philip sends his best wishes for continued success."

The *Daily Mirror* weighed in on the debate as to whether the Beatles were still as popular, with the prescient observation: "Beatlemania days are over, not because fans have lost interest, but because the Beatles are tired of whistle-stop tours."

The pace was truly exhausting and it was no surprise that the Beatles would not undertake such a schedule again.

Following a brief holiday in May (John and George to Tahiti; Paul and Ringo to the Virgin Isles), a phenomenally successful tour of Australia in June saw the biggest-ever crowds assemble to see the Beatles. The summer was taken up with the group's first major trek across North America, where A *Hard Day's Night* had opened simultaneously in 500 cinemas on 11th August, as well as a British tour in the autumn, culminating at the end of the year with a repeat of the Beatles' Christmas Show, this time at the Hammersmith Odeon. (A proposed tour of South Africa in November was cancelled as the Beatles refused to play to segregated audiences.)

On top of all that, on days off from the touring schedule, the Beatles taped enough material for their fourth album, *Beatles For Sale*, and latest single, 'I Feel Fine'/ 'She's A Woman',

YEAH YEAH! YEAH! TODAY'S BEATLE'S FANS ARE TOMORROW'S BASEBALL FANS

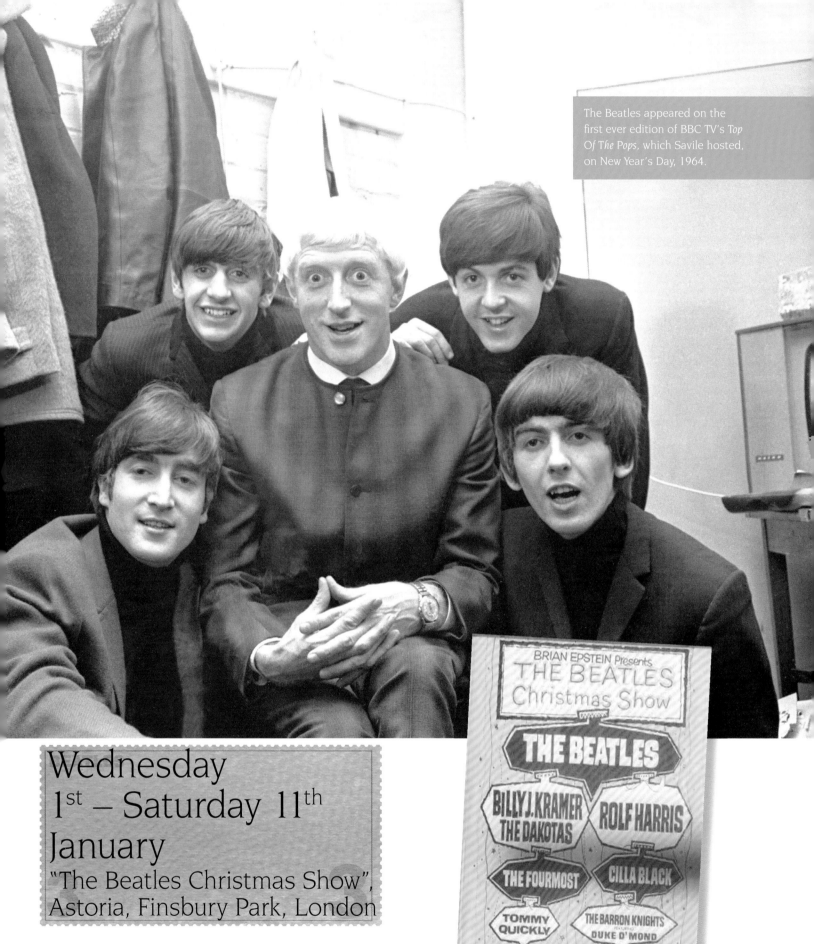

The Beatles appeared on the first ever edition of BBC TV's *Top Of The Pops*, which Savile hosted, on New Year's Day, 1964.

Wednesday
1st – Saturday 11th January
"The Beatles Christmas Show", Astoria, Finsbury Park, London

Almost 100,000 people attended 30 performances at this 3,000-seat venue, later reopened in the early Seventies as one of London's premier rock theatres, the Rainbow. The only mishap was John's Gibson Jumbo acoustic guitar being stolen from a backstage dressing room, and it was never recovered.

BRIAN EPSTEIN presents
THE BEATLES Christmas Show

THE BEATLES

BILLY J. KRAMER THE DAKOTAS   **ROLF HARRIS**

THE FOURMOST   **CILLA BLACK**

TOMMY QUICKLY   **THE BARRON KNIGHTS** FEATURING **DUKE D'MOND**

DEVISED AND PRODUCED BY PETER YOLLAND

FINSBURY PARK ASTORIA

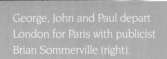

George, John and Paul depart
London for Paris with publicist
Brian Sommerville (right).

Tuesday 14ᵗʰ January

John, Paul, George, Brian Epstein, Mal Evans and Beatles press representative Brian Sommerville left London for Paris (without Ringo who, fog-bound in Liverpool, followed a day later via London, accompanied by Neil Aspinall). Arriving at Le Bourget Airport (John wearing his Mary Quant-designed leather cap and dark glasses), the group gave a chaotic press conference at the airport before being driven to the George V Hotel by chauffeur Bill Corbett, where they checked in to their palatial £50-a-night suite.

While George went out to visit the Eiffel Tower and on to a nighclub, John and Paul met Bruno Coquatrix, the manager of L'Olympia Theatre, and a representative from Odeon Records, the Beatles' label in France, before settling down at the piano that had been specially moved into their suite, to work on song ideas mainly destined for the soundtrack to A Hard Day's Night.

The Beatles meet the press (and customs officers) at Le Bourget, Paris.

Wednesday 15th January
Cinema Cyrano, Versailles, France

During the morning, before Ringo's arrival, the three Beatles brought the Champs-Elysées to a standstill when they wandered along part of the famous thoroughfare to sightsee, trailed by a horde of press and fans. The Beatles were already known to some in France as "the English group with the French hairstyles".

At the Versailles concert – a warm-up for the Olympia season – a fan jumped on stage and danced away next to John before being removed by Mal Evans.

The Beatles were quick to notice the differences compared with British audiences – namely that female screams of adoration were replaced by roars of approval from a mainly male audience and that the group could actually be heard.

Set-list: 'Roll Over Beethoven', 'From Me To You', 'I Saw Her Standing There', 'This Boy', 'Boys', 'I Want To Hold Your Hand', 'Till There Was You', 'She Loves You', 'Twist And Shout' and an encore of 'Long Tall Sally'.

However, their impression of Paris got completely knocked for six when the news came through at 3am from London that, in less than three weeks after its release, 'I Want To Hold Your Hand' had reached No. 1 on the national American Billboard chart, becoming the fastest-rising disc by any British artiste in the States, with sales surpassing a million, 10,000 copies a day selling in New York alone. Mal gave the boys piggyback rides around their suite in a party that lasted until dawn. It was, arguably, the most momentous highlight in the Beatles' career.

Les Garcons! The Beatles' French audiences were mainly male.

The Beatles pose on a balcony
at the George V Hotel.

Thursday 16th January – Tuesday 4th February
A three-week season at L'Olympia Theatre, Paris

3

Trini Lopez topped the bill in the first half, while Sylvie Vartan opened the second half before the Beatles. Ticket prices were expensive; the cheapest seats being 15 shillings.

On the opening night, Mal Evans had to contend with three power failures as the amps fell silent and a backstage punch-up with photographers fighting to get into the Beatles'

dressing room, having refused to obey the "no photos" edict.

French Beatles' fans mingled with the more glitzy Parisian patrons who were sedate and politely clapped in time. The following night went down better, with the first teenage, mainly male, audience shouting their appreciation. As the Beatles' popularity grew, many who held genuine tickets were kept out of the theatre, while some found their seats had been taken and had to watch the show standing in the stalls. On the 19th one of three shows that day was broadcast live by French radio station Europe 1.

The set-list included: 'From Me To You', 'This Boy', 'I Want To Hold Your Hand', 'She Loves You' and 'Twist And Shout'. Reviews were mixed, with one paper (*Parisien Libere*) saying the Beatles' music was "daddy's rock 'n' roll stuff. Nothing very new".

The Beatles got around the City of Light without too much bother; sightseeing at Montmarte and stopping by the Blues

John goes cap in hand for spare francs outside the George V.

Cherchez le femme: The Beatles
with Sylvie Vartan.

The Beatles onstage at the Paris Olympia.

The Beatles were obviously not *de rigeur* to some of the Olympia's older patrons.

Paul, John & George harmonize on 'This Boy'.

Club where Memphis Slim was performing. (They politely declined an offer to jam with the blues legend.)

On the 28th, a day off, John and George flew back to London, attending a party in honour of the Ronettes who were currently touring Britain, with the girls' legendary producer Phil Spector playing chaperone.

Back in Paris the following day, at EMI's Pathé Marconi Studios, the Beatles reluctantly recorded German-language versions of 'She Loves You' and 'I Want To Hold Your Hand' for the German market, as well as the A-side of their next single, 'Can't Buy Me Love', completed at EMI Studios on 25th February, released 20th March, to advance orders of 1 million.

Wednesday
5th February
3

The Beatles returned from Paris to London Airport at 1pm to a screaming welcome from truant schoolgirls. When told by an ITN reporter about criticism from Detroit university students that the Beatles' haircuts were un-American, John quipped, "That's very observant of them because we aren't American".

The Beatles leave for New York; (right) with a posse of British press and photographers including Dezo Hoffman (behind Ringo) and *Liverpool Echo* journalist George Harrison (top right).

Friday 7th February

At 11am the Beatles departed London Airport for New York on Pan-Am Flight 101. Travelling in their entourage was Brian Epstein, Neil Aspinall, Mal Evans and a posse of British newspapermen (including, of course, representatives from the *Mirror*), Cavern owner Ray McFall and Phil Spector.

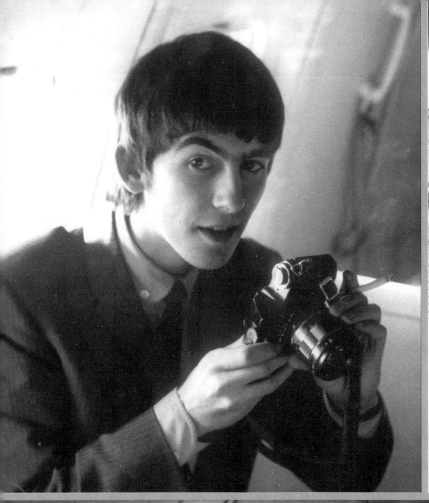

Cynthia Lennon: "It was a memorable plane ride because the whole of the British press were with us and the boys were all performing for the press so it was click here, click there and pose here and pose there. There was lots of drink going along and lots of excitement."

As the Boeing 707 touched down at John F. Kennedy International Airport at 1.20pm New York time, the Beatles originally thought the uproarious noise they could hear was for somebody else's arrival. After all, as they had told the press on the flight, "America has all the best music. Why should they want us?" As the Beatles emerged down the aircraft steps, they were met by over 100 photographers and newspapermen and an almighty roar from over 3,000 waiting fans, the first of whom gathered at 4am, many wearing

Top: John wearing his glasses that he normally removed for photos.
Bottom: John and Cynthia Lennon with record producer Phil Spector.

The Beatles' cases get a close inspection from US customs men while (bottom) not every American male became a Beatles fan overnight.

BEATLES ARE STARVING THE BARBERS

ENGLAND GET OUT OF IRELAND

BEATLE UNFAIR to BALD ME

Beatles sweatshirts and T-shirts thanks to Capitol's advance publicity campaign. An airport official was heard to remark, "We've never seen anything like this here before. Never. Not even for kings and queens".

After clearing customs, the first of the usual Beatles press conferences took place in a room ill-equipped to handle the mass of over 200 photographers and newsmen who jostled to get nearer. Tempers were lost and a typically flustered Brian Sommerville (who had flown out in advance the day before) appealed for quiet. George took it all in his stride. "Let the feasting begin," he called.

Seizing his moment, brash, fast-talking New York DJ Murray Kaufman (a.k.a. Murray the K) of Radio WINS, ingratiated himself with the group. "Tell Murray the K to cut out the crap," one embittered journo yelled.

"Cut out the crap, Murray!" the Beatles repeated, laughing. Whether they liked it or not, Kaufman was now part of their entourage. As Sommerville called for the first question, the hard-bitten, cynical New York press, there to destroy these Limey bugs, simply melted on the tide of the typically cute Beatles charm and wit that followed.

The Beatles' first American press conference with Murray the K (in fur hat) hovering below.

"What do you think of the comment that you're nothing but a bunch of British Elvis Presleys?"

Ringo: "It's not true… it's not true" (giving a reasonable Elvis hip-swivel).

"Would you please sing something?"

All: "No!"

"There's some doubt that you can sing."

John: "No, we need money first."

"How many of you are bald that you have to wear those wigs?"

Paul: "I'm bald – don't tell anyone please."

John: "We're all bald – and deaf and dumb, too."

"Are you going to get a haircut at all while you're here?"

George: "I had one yesterday…"

Ringo: "That's no lie, it's true – you should have seen him the day before!"

"What do you think your music does for these people?"

Ringo: "It pleases them, I think – it must do because they're buying it."

"Why does it excite them so much?"

Paul: "We don't know, really…"

John: "If we knew, we'd form another group and be the managers."

After the conference was declared over, the Beatles fought their way out to four separate Cadillacs limos for the drive into the city. On the way, they were astonished to hear radio stations broadcasting the time in Beatle minutes, giving Beatle weather reports as well as military-style updates on their arrival, all linked by non-stop Beatles music. It must have seemed surreal to four young musicians from a provincial British seaport, who had grown up on American culture and yet now, the Yanks couldn't get enough of *them*.

The convoy arrived at the plush Plaza Hotel on Fifth

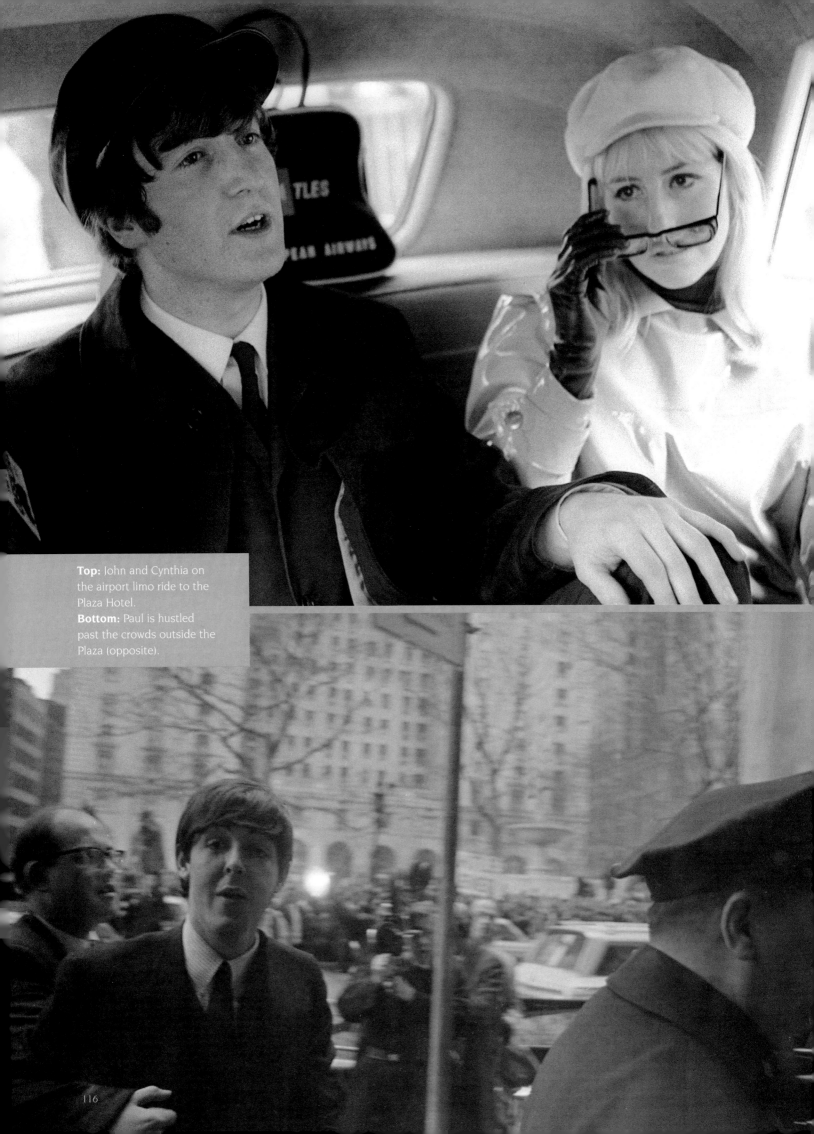

Top: John and Cynthia on the airport limo ride to the Plaza Hotel.
Bottom: Paul is hustled past the crowds outside the Plaza (opposite).

Avenue at Central Park South at 4pm – just as schools were finishing for the week. The management were horrified to see the bedlam caused outside their august establishment – the bookings had been made the previous November when John Lennon, Paul McCartney, George Harrison and Richard Starkey were assumed to be four English businessmen.

The Beatles were ensconced in their suite on the 12th floor, all on one corridor sealed off by guards from the Burns Detective Agency. Outside, 100 of New York City's finest were on standby, backed up by mounted police, for whenever the Beatles were due to leave the hotel.

Imprisoned in their suite, with only journalists and a camera crew for company (both Granada Television and the Maysles Brothers were documenting events for a cinema *verité*- style documentary called *What's Happening: The Beatles In The USA*), the Beatles indulged in the sort of wit and japery that would find its way into *A Hard Day's Night*, calling up radio stations to make requests and listening, fascinated, to the music that poured endlessly from the AM transmitters to their portable transistor radios. In England, where pop music was strictly rationed by "needle time" over the staid BBC airwaves, this was a totally new situation for the group.

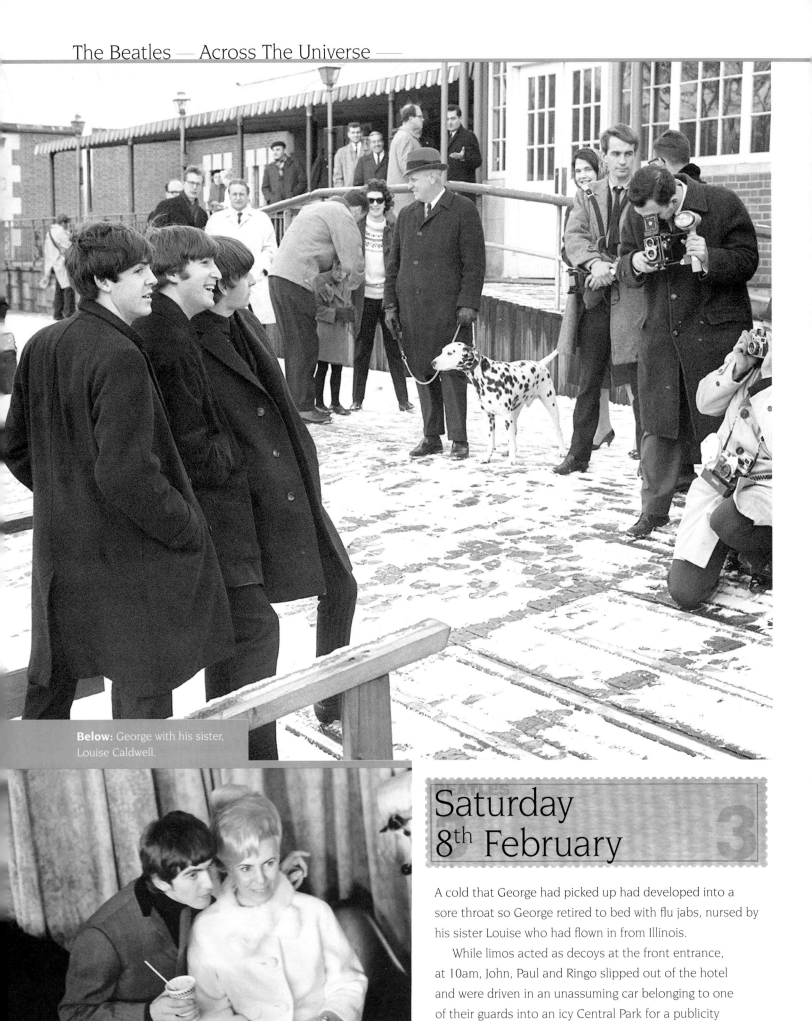

Below: George with his sister, Louise Caldwell.

Saturday
8th February

A cold that George had picked up had developed into a sore throat so George retired to bed with flu jabs, nursed by his sister Louise who had flown in from Illinois.

While limos acted as decoys at the front entrance, at 10am, John, Paul and Ringo slipped out of the hotel and were driven in an unassuming car belonging to one of their guards into an icy Central Park for a publicity photo session.

The Beatles in Central Park – note the ever-present transistor radio.

From the park, the Beatles were driven straight to CBS TV Studio 50 at Broadway and 53rd Street in time for 1.30pm rehearsals for the following day's *Ed Sullivan Show*. Before any work could begin the Beatles first had to fill out the appropriate forms to join the AFM (American Federation of Musicians). For the initial camera tests, Neil Aspinall filled in for George until the real thing arrived – hauled temporarily from his sickbed – to take up position.

Bernie Ilson (*Ed Sullivan Show* publicity man):
"*They were the most professional rock musicians I had ever met. They came in three hours before the regular rehearsal to sit with the soundman to get the right balance. Ed Sullivan paid the Beatles $10,000 for the first three shows. At the time, a top act could earn $7,500 for one appearance.*"
Deborah Levitt (*original New York fan*): "*Security was tight but for a moment when the door was unguarded I got in to the theatre. Being a fan for two years prior, I had to get in. It was phenomenal, especially the rehearsal where there were so many people, press, photographers and security people.*"

After the rehearsals, John, Paul and Ringo were taken to dine at the exclusive 21 Club on West 52nd Street by Capitol executives and went on a sightseeing trip around town by car. George meanwhile was back resting at the Plaza, talking to journalists and radio stations, and accepting a gift – a new 12-string guitar presented to him by a representative from Rickenbacker. John also received a new Rickenbacker model from the guitar company.

Sunday 9th February

The day was spent at the CBS theatre, rehearsing for the live *Ed Sullivan Show* broadcast that night as well as pre-taping an afternoon appearance for a *Sullivan* show due to air on 23rd February, after the Beatles returned to Britain. Over 50,000 fans had applied for the 728 available seats in the theatre. The Beatles first pre-taped their 23rd February segment, performing three numbers: 'Twist And Shout', 'Please Please Me' and 'I Want To Hold Your Hand'.

For the evening's broadcast, networked across America from 8 to 9pm, following Sullivan's introduction, the Beatles performed 'All My Loving', 'Till There Was You' and 'She Loves You', returning in the second half as the penultimate act to deliver 'I Saw Her Standing There' and 'I Want To Hold Your Hand'. If there could be one defining moment for Beatlemania in America, it was the Beatles' first appearance on *The Ed Sullivan Show*.

For American baby boomers, the memory of seeing the Beatles' *Ed Sullivan* debut is as clear as where they were when hearing the news of John F. Kennedy's assassination. It was the Beatles' appearance that helped lift the country out of its doldrums in the months following the loss of the young president. Sullivan called the Beatles "tremendous ambassadors of goodwill".

As popular legend records, the crime rate across the country fell as it seemed the entire population – or 73 million of the American television viewing audience, at least – tuned in to watch the Beatles, surpassing the previous world record

for the largest-ever TV audience. The group were delighted
to receive among the well-wishing telegrams one from Elvis
Presley and his manager, Colonel Tom Parker, which read,
"Congratulations on your appearance on *The Ed Sullivan Show*
and your visit to America. We hope your engagement will be a
successful one and your visit pleasant."

Following the live transmission, the Beatles were whisked
back to the Plaza where Murray the K offered to show John,
Paul and Ringo around the clubs – first the Playboy on 59th
Street and then on to the world-renowned Peppermint Lounge
(the home of the Twist), followed by the press and the Maysles
cameras, before calling it a night at 4am.

The following day, all four Beatles met the press at the
Plaza and were presented with two Gold Discs from Capitol
Records president, Alan Livingston, for the 'I Want To Hold
Your Hand' single and *Meet The Beatles* album. No access was
considered too great and the Beatles did round after round of
interviews for print, radio and film.

Tuesday 11th February
Washington Coliseum, Washington DC

3

With snowstorms blanketing the East Coast, and mindful of the fate that had met their hero Buddy Holly five years earlier, the Beatles insisted on travelling by train from Penn Station to Washington. The Pennsylvania Railroad Company attached a special reserved coach to their express Congressman, stopping en route at Delaware, Newark and Baltimore. On board the train was the ever-present press contingent who followed the Beatles' every move, as well as a few lucky fans.

Arriving in heavy snow, the Beatles were hurried along to cars which drove them straight to the empty Coliseum for the customary press conference and interviews. One of these was with local DJ Carroll James of WWDC, the first American disc jockey to play an imported copy of 'I Want To Hold Your Hand' on 17th December 1963. The group then stepped outside for a photo session – with Capitol Hill looming in the background – as well as indulging in a staged snowball fight.

The Beatles then retired to the seventh floor of the Shoreham Hotel that had been given over to their entourage. One family had refused to move so the management resorted to subterfuge – shutting down all the facilities and explaining there'd been a power failure before they got the message.

Mal Evans sets up the Beatles' equipment at the Washington Coliseum.

The Beatles are put on show at the British Embassy ball in Washington.

The Beatles' first American concert, held on a boxing ring stage awkwardly situated in the middle of the audience, was seen by 8,600. Also appearing were the Caravelles, Tommy Roe, and the Chiffons. The Beatles were forced to make a well-protected dash through the crowd to get to the stage and then after every few numbers, with the help of Mal Evans, moved their equipment around to face various sections of the surrounding audience.

Set-list: 'Roll Over Beethoven', 'From Me To You', 'I Saw Her Standing There', 'This Boy', 'All My Loving', 'I Wanna Be Your Man', 'Please Please Me', 'Till There Was You', 'She Loves You', 'I Want To Hold Your Hand', 'Twist And Shout' and 'Long Tall Sally'.

Watched proudly from the back of the arena by Brian Epstein, the concert was filmed on videotape by CBS and later blown up to film for screening at closed-circuit cinemas across America the following month.

That evening the Beatles were put on show for a graceless bunch of society Hooray Henrys at the British Embassy masked charity ball, thrown by the Ambassador Sir David and Lady Ormsby-Gore. After one souvenir-hunting "animal", as John Lennon described them, snipped off a lock of Ringo's hair, the Beatles beat a retreat back to their hotel at 1am, angrily requesting that Epstein not accede to such requests again.

Wednesday 12th February
Carnegie Hall, New York

The Beatles returned by train to Penn Station to mob scenes at the terminal and Plaza Hotel, with twice as many fans around because it was Lincoln's Birthday. To prevent the problem experienced in getting the group into the front entrance, the Beatles sneaked out via a back elevator and through the kitchens into taxis taking them to Carnegie Hall on West 57th Street.

The Beatles gave two performances (7.45 and 11.15pm – set list as for Washington – for which they received $7,000) at this prestigious venue, which had sold all 5,000 seats within 24 hours of the box office opening on Monday 27th January. An additional 50 seats for more reserved patrons were arranged on the stage to accommodate the booking overflow. George Martin was present with Capitol representatives to see about recording the shows – a plan that was thwarted by union officials from the AFM. (Martin was able to record Shirley Bassey's performance at the venue three nights later.)

In assessing the Beatles appeal, a *New York Times* journalist attempted to describe the phenomenon: "Multiply Elvis Presley by four, subtract six years from his age, add British accents and a sharp sense of humour – and the answer is the Beatles, yeah, yeah, yeah."

The promoter of the Carnegie shows, Sid Bernstein, had offered Brian Epstein $15,000 for the Beatles to play an extra show at Madison Square Garden but Brian declined the offer, not wishing to risk overexposure.

ON THE SCENE

Photographed by United Press
International Candid Camera Team. **EXCLUSIVE**

THE
BEATLES
AT CARNEGIE HALL

Written by RALPH COSHAM in New York
Over 60 Illustrations   A Panther Pictorial   2/6

135

John being interviewed by DJ Murray the K on the flight to Miami.

Thursday 13th February

The Beatles flew to Miami at 1.30pm, arriving at 4pm to blue skies and a frenzied crowd of between 6,000 to 8,000 girls who shattered windows and broke fences to get a glimpse of them. The group had flown down in tourist class because a hoaxer had changed their flight arrangements without their knowledge – hence another journey accompanied by eager journalists, autograph hunters and Murray the K. The Beatles were given a police motorcycle escort for the journey to the Deauville Hotel at Miami Beach.

Shortly before midnight the Beatles slipped out of their hotel and were taken in cars driven by Miami police to visit the area's famed strip of hotels and bars. They first went to a nightclub and sat for 45 minutes sipping whisky and cokes, listening to the house band and watching young Americans twist. Then several customers asked for autographs so the Beatles left for the Castaways club. However, it only took a short while for them to be recognized there also and without ordering a drink, they stood up and left. According to news reports, there was an argument outside between the Beatles and their road managers. John Lennon said, "I thought you said we were on holiday". The Beatles then roared off, with one car being used as a decoy to shake off the following press. The Beatles party arrived back at the Deauville at about 1.30 am.

The Beatles pose in a pool for a LIFE magazine cover story.

Friday 14th February

In contrast to New York's freezing temperatures, the Beatles spent the day in 85-degree heat relaxing on the luxury yacht *Southern Trail*, offered for their use by owner Mr Bernard Castro. Before embarking on a trip around the Bay of Miami, a special photo session in a swimming pool was arranged for the cover of LIFE magazine – a singular honour in American entertainment. The Beatles accepted a dinner invitation at the home of their personal police bodyguard, Sgt. Buddy Dresner. Following their return to the Deauville they caught comedian Don Rickell's floor show at the hotel – he spent the evening cracking cheap gags at their expense – and the others (minus John) also saw comedian Myron Cohen and dancer Carol Lawrence.

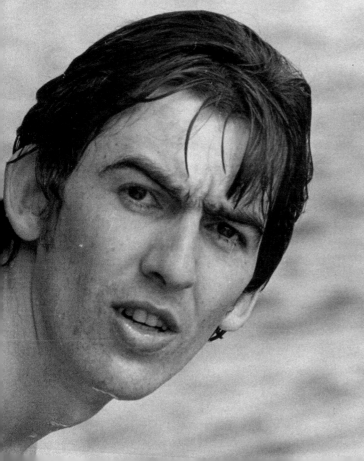

Saturday
15th February

A full day's rehearsal for the Beatles' second appearance on *The Ed Sullivan Show*, in which they co-starred with Mitzi Gaynor, and which went ahead despite a bomb hoax. A "dry run" was taped at 2pm before an eager studio audience of 2,600.

Sunday 16th February

The producers of *The Ed Sullivan Show* had issued 3,500 tickets though the theatre inside the Deauville held less than this capacity, causing uproar when people holding valid tickets were refused admission. Among the audience were Joe Louis and Sonny Liston (the latter preparing for his heavyweight bout against Cassius Clay on 25th February. The Beatles made a heavily publicized visit to Clay at his Miami gym on 18th February).

The Beatles performed 'She Loves You', 'This Boy' and 'All My Loving' in the first half of the show and 'I Saw Her Standing There', 'From Me To You' and 'I Want To Hold Your Hand' in the second half.

Brian Epstein was impressed enough to describe the Beatles' performance as the "best they have ever made on television", but the Beatles (and critics) were disappointed with the sound on both the New York and Miami TV appearances. Mr Maurice Lansberg, the owner of the Deauville, threw a party for the Beatles, Sullivan and the rest of the show's cast and technicians.

Instead of returning to London as planned, the Beatles stayed on in Miami until the end of the week. A London charity luncheon they had been due to attend on Thursday 20th February in aid of Oxfam was postponed to early March (and even then the Beatles were too busy to attend).

During the rest of their well-earned break, the Beatles attended a drive-in movie (seeing Elvis Presley's *Fun In Acapulco*) as well as enjoying swimming, water-skiing, fishing and generally relaxing, while John and Paul finished work on the soundtrack songs for *A Hard Day's Night*.

Saturday 22nd February

The Beatles flew from Miami to New York and then caught Pan-Am flight 102 back to London, arriving home at 8.10am to an estimated 12,000 fans, many of whom had camped out all night to make sure of good positions to greet their conquering heroes. One London Airport official, who had seen arrivals there over the last 12 years, said, "There's never been anything like this. It was absolutely unprecedented! We thought perhaps 1,000 would turn up, and although we've not been able to get an accurate number we think there were 6,000. Fortunately, there have been no serious casualties."

John Lennon was moved to comment, "America was great, but this reception tops everything". Asked on landing whether they had a special message for the prime minister and their parents, the Beatles shot back, "Hello Alec, Hello, mum".

Daily Mirror

3d. Saturday, February 22, 1964   No. 18,716

WELCOME HOME BEATLES!

SPECIAL!

THE Mirror — and you—say "Welcome home!" to the Beatles.

If you can't "hold their hands," hold up this page so that they can see the headline!

By ROBIN PARKIN

THE Beatles were flying home . . . and building up all through last night was the greatest "welcome home" London Airport has ever seen.

By 2 o'clock this

ALL-NIGHT SIEGE AT LONDON AIRPORT

morning, bewildered airport police were trying to calm down 1,000 worshipping fans.

There were amazing scenes, like the one pictured above, as the girls chanted "Beatle, Beatle, Beatle."

They waved Beatle pictures, Beatle banners, Beatle hats—even a "Wel-

come Home Beatles" banner made from daffodils.

Winter holidaymakers and tourists stared open mouthed at the carnival on the main building's carpeted balcony as the girls sang the Beatles' hit songs.

One policeman mopped his brow and said: "Blimey, I've never seen a show like this—and the Beatles aren't even here yet."

The balcony was like a

giant camp. Girls stretched out on the carpet talking of nothing but Ringo, John, Paul and George.

And police were told to prepare for eleven coachloads of fans from Liverpool, and another sixteen coaches from the Midlands and the South.

One moment of drama, and one only, silenced the screaming girls.

That was when 15-year-

old Linda Biggs of East Ham dropped an iced beetle-shaped cake on the airport stairs.

Amid gasps of horror Linda collapsed in tears—but the cake was only slightly damaged.

The night wore on. Still the fans came, and at least

6,000 teenagers were expected to turn up for breakfast-time with the Beatles.

The gathering of the fans had begun shortly before midnight, then a steady stream turned the second floor of the main passenger terminal into a "refugee camp."

Blankets were unrolled, food parcels unpacked, and

Continued on Back Page.

More pictures on Back Page

THE EMPIRE POOL AND SPORTS ARENA, WEMBLEY
APRIL 26
ADMIT AT SOUTH DOOR

MAURICE KINN presents the ANNUAL
"NEW MUSICAL EXPRESS"
POLL WINNERS CONCERT
SUNDAY, APRIL 26th, 1964
at 2.30 p.m.   Doors open 2 p.m.

ENTRANCE
73

SOUTH GRAND TIER
25/-

ROW E
SEAT 80

TO BE RETAINED

MAURICE KINN PRESENTS
THE
new MUSICAL EXPRESS
1963-64
ANNUAL
POLL-WINNERS
ALL-STAR
CONCERT
SUNDAY
APRIL 26th 1964

EMPIRE POOL WEMBLEY
OFFICIAL PROGRAMME
PRICE 1/-

Sunday 26th April
NME Poll Winners Concert, Empire Pool, Wembley, London

The Beatles' first live set in over two months came with their bill-topping appearance before an audience of 10,000 at this annual event organized by the *New Musical Express*. (The Beatles had appeared with much less fanfare at the previous year's event on Sunday 21st April.)

Introduced by a visiting Murray the K, the Beatles performed 'She Loves You', 'You Can't Do That' (such was the break from the stage, John managed to forget where he was in both songs), 'Twist And Shout', 'Long Tall Sally' and 'Can't Buy Me Love', their latest single which had just slipped down to second in chart position, its place taken by 'A World Without Love' by Peter and Gordon, written by none other than Lennon and McCartney.

The Beatles returned to the stage briefly to receive their awards in the 1963/64 poll from *The Saint* actor, Roger Moore for Second British Small Group, Top British Vocal Group, Top Four Records Of The Year and the World's Leading Vocal Group.

Receiving NME poll awards from Roger Moore (right).

WE WANT THE BEATLES

THIS PETITION HAS BEEN CIRCULATED IN EDINBURGH FOR 10 DAYS. IT IS 12 FEET LONG AND HAS BEEN SIGNED BY OVER 7000 BEATLES FANS WHO WERE VERY DISAPPOINTED WHEN THE CAPITAL WAS MISSED OUT DURING THEIR SCOTTISH TOUR.

DJ David Jacobs shows off the petition that brought the Beatles to Edinburgh.
Below: A startled looking George and Paul wave a greeting to the Scottish capital.
Right: The Beatles with the Lord Provost.

Wednesday 29th April
ABC Cinema, Edinburgh

3

The Beatles flew up on a chartered flight from Ruislip Airport to start a brief Scottish tour (playing Glasgow Odeon the following night). When first announced by promoter Albert Bonici in December, the Beatles' Scottish concerts were scheduled to be a week of shows in Glasgow followed by a one-nighter at Edinburgh's Playhouse Theatre. The Scottish capital was added to the Beatles' itinerary after a massive 10,000-signature petition was circulated beseeching them to play there because the city had been missed out on their Scottish tour the previous October.

During a press reception, the astonished Beatles were asked to donate £100,000 by the Lord Provost, Duncan Weatherstone, towards the Edinburgh International Festival. "I am not joking," Weatherstone said. "I thought they might like to help other aspects of music and art."

"It was a good try but we haven't got any loose change," John quipped.

Paul added, "We hear he tries this with everybody!"

Sunday 31st May
Pops Alive! Prince of Wales Theatre, London

After four weeks of holidays the Beatles returned to live work with two sell-out shows (6 and 8.30pm), announced back in February, at this Brian Epstein-promoted event – part of a series of Sunday concerts by NEMS-managed artists. It was also a return to the venue where the Beatles had triumphed in last year's Royal Variety Show.

Set-list included 'Can't Buy Me Love', 'All My Loving', 'This Boy', 'Roll Over Beethoven', 'Till There Was You', 'Twist And Shout' and 'Long Tall Sally'.

The Beatles rehearsing with Jimmy Nicol at EMI Studios. John and George look less than happy with the arrangement.

Thursday 4th June

The Beatles left for the first leg of a world tour, joined for the first and only time in their touring career by a stand-in after Ringo had collapsed with laryngitis during a photo session in London the previous day and been admitted to University College Hospital.

Following a phone call from George Martin, Jimmy Nicol, currently the drummer for Georgie Fame and the Blue Flames, agreed to sit in for a fee of £500, wearing Ringo's stage suits and playing his kit. After a brief afternoon rehearsal at EMI Studios, the following morning he flew with the Beatles to Copenhagen where they were met by over 6,000 fans at Kastrup Airport.

Following shows at the K.B. Hallen, inside the Tivoli Gardens, the Fab Three and Jimmy flew on to Holland, taping a TV show at Treslong in Hillegom on the 5th and playing two shows the following night at an auction hall in Blokker.

Sunday 7th June

The Beatles returned to London on a morning flight where they were met by John's Aunt Mimi, who accompanied her nephew on the 16-hour BOAC flight to Hong Kong to start the group's tour of the Far East, Australia and New Zealand. Liverpudlian air hostess, Anne Creech, who is seen running a large comb through George's mop, was assigned to the Beatles' flight to make the lads "feel at home".

Thursday 2ⁿᵈ July

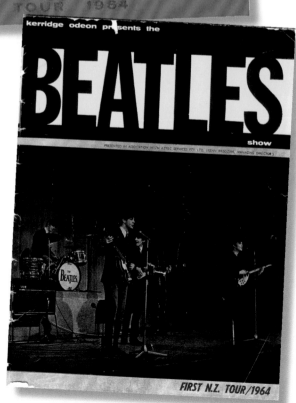

The Beatles arrived back at London Airport via Singapore and Frankfurt at 11.10am to just 200 fans, one of whom said, "We knew nothing about it until the last moment. Anyway it's a school day, isn't it?"

There to meet her husband after a month away was Cynthia Lennon, who remained blissfully unaware of the excesses that often characterized an overseas Beatles' tour, which John later compared to Fellini's *Satyricon* "with four musicians going through it".

The Beatles' Australian tour was full of great triumphs – nearly 1,000 bid a sodden greeting in torrential rain at Sydney's Mascot Airport on 11ᵗʰ June, while the next day in Adelaide over 300,000 people gathered on the route from the airport to the group's hotel in the centre of the city – the biggest crowd ever assembled to see the Beatles at any time in their careers. Roughly the same number congregated in

Melbourne on 14th June where Ringo was reunited with his fellow Beatles (and Jimmy Nicol promptly slipped back into obscurity). Throughout Australia, people of all ages gathered in an almighty crush of humanity to see these four musicians who had taken on an unearthly quality.

Reporter: "*Did you know your welcome was bigger than what the Queen had got?*"
George: "*Perhaps the Queen should have cut a few good records.*"
Reporter: "*How long will you stay a Beatle?*"

John: "*Well, I won't be singing 'Twist And Shout' when I'm 30.*"

The end of the tour was marred by some Beatles-haters pelting the group with eggs when they made balcony appearances in Christchurch and Brisbane. When Beatles publicist Derek Taylor arranged a meeting between the group and Queensland University representatives of the egg-throwing brigade to ask them to explain their actions, the student delegation said that the barrage was a protest against materialism and that the Beatles were a product of advertising.

Sunday 19th July
ABC Theatre, Blackpool

3

John, Paul and Ringo flew up to the Lancashire seaside resort of Blackpool the previous day (George elected to motor up in his new E-type Jaguar) to rehearse for their live bill-topping appearance on the popular hour-long, Sunday night variety programme *Blackpool Night Out*, broadcast live from the ABC

Theatre at 8.25pm. Other guests appearing that week were dancer Chita Rivera, Frank Berry, Jimmy Edwards, and Lionel Blair and His Dancers.

As well as the expected comedy sketches – the Beatles as surgeons and dustmen! – the group plugged in to perform live versions of 'A Hard Day's Night', 'Things We Said Today', 'You Can't Do That', 'If I Fell' (John introduced the song by indicating "to prove we're not miming"), and 'Long Tall Sally'.

Ringo, John and Paul arrive in Blackpool. Beatles' publicist Derek Taylor stands at right.

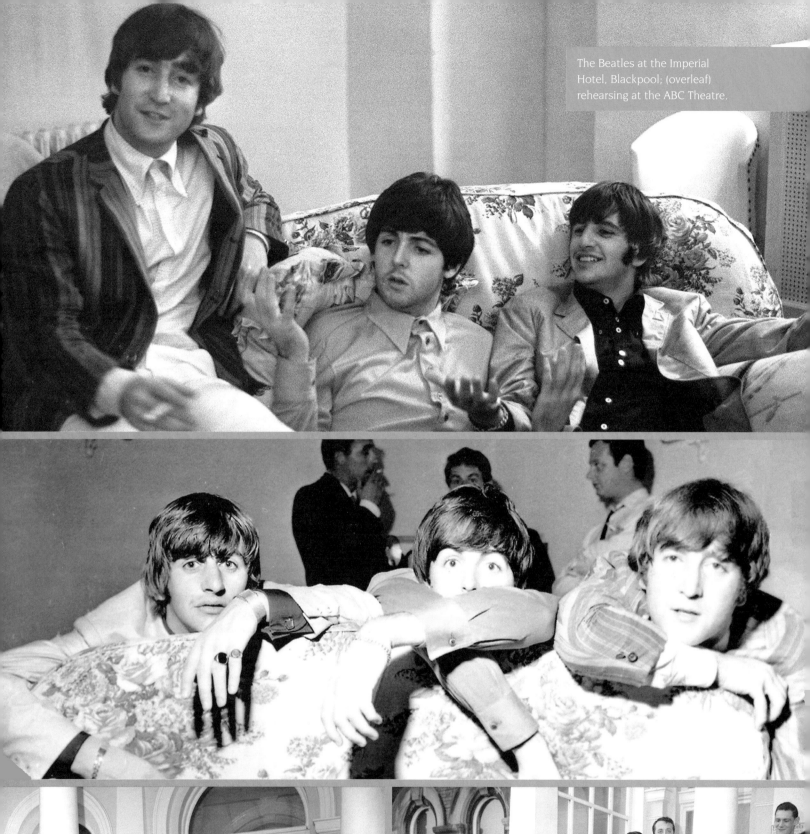

The Beatles at the Imperial Hotel, Blackpool; (overleaf) rehearsing at the ABC Theatre.

Thursday 30th July

The Beatles returned to London Airport from their second visit to Sweden – playing four shows over two nights in Stockholm at an ice hockey arena. A total of 6,500 attended the first show but as the second performance was at 10pm – too late for youngsters – the venue was only half-full. During the opening show, John and Paul received electric shocks from unearthed microphones.

Sunday 9th August
Futurist Theatre, Scarborough

Brian Epstein had booked the Beatles into a series of summer Sunday shows at British seaside towns – the first of these was at Brighton's Hippodrome on 12th July, followed by Blackpool's Opera House (26th July) and Bournemouth's Gaumont Cinema (2nd August). Support acts at this Scarborough appearance

(two shows 6.25 and 8.45) were David Macbeth, Cherry Roland, the Plus Fours with Erky Grant, Johnny Peters and the JPs, and compere Dick Francis.

The Beatles landed at RAF Leconfield, 25 miles from the holiday resort on the Yorkshire coast, and drove to South Bay in a limousine. Approaching the Futurist Theatre, around 2,000 fans engulfed the car, trapping it near the side entrance so only John was able to open his door and flee inside. The other three had to vault the front bonnet to safety with the aid of a police officer.

Sunday 16th August
Opera House, Blackpool

3

The last of the summer concerts was memorable in that the supporting bill featured two of the Sixties' other major acts, the Kinks (who had recently supported the Beatles in Bournemouth on 2nd August and had just released their first No. 1 hit single in 'You Really Got Me') and The High Numbers, an interim name for the Who.

John Entwistle: "The Opera House was one of those old-fashioned theatres with speakers in the dressing room so you could hear the other artists performing. Because of all the constant screaming, nobody could hear what the Beatles were singing anyway. All that was coming through these speakers were the words, and some of them were hilarious. The Hard Day's Night film had just come out and Lennon was singing, 'It's been a hard day's night and I've been wanking like a dog!' The audience couldn't hear it but we could."

The Beatles make a mad dash from the ABC, Blackpool.

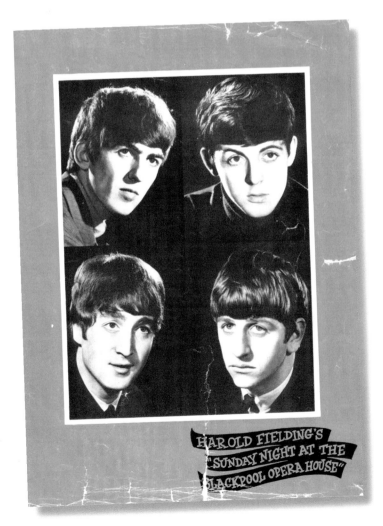

HAROLD FIELDING'S "SUNDAY NIGHT AT THE BLACKPOOL OPERA HOUSE"

At noon the Beatles left London Airport on a 13-hour, 6,000-mile Pan-Am flight to America, with brief stops in Winnipeg and Los Angeles, before arriving at San Francisco International Airport at 6.24pm local time.

The Beatles' second North American visit (their first proper nationwide tour) involved 32 shows in 24 cities over five weeks, travelling some 40,000 miles, playing to more than half a million. In the modern age of touring rock 'n' roll juggernauts with large entourages it seems ludicrous now to think that the Beatles were accompanied on a major tour by just two road managers (Neil Aspinall, Mal Evans) and a press officer (Derek Taylor).

At San Francisco, the Beatles were originally to receive a ticker-tape welcome in an open car – usually only given to royalty and heads of state – followed by a civic reception. However, with the recent Kennedy assassination in mind, and already fully aware of how far Beatlemania had got out of hand, George Harrison refused to go along with the plan. Instead, the Beatles disembarked and two limousines drove them 50 yards to a specially erected 25-foot square platform known as "Beatlesville", three-quarters of a mile north-west of the main terminal, surrounded by a 5-foot cyclone fence.

The Beatles were due to speak but when the crush against the wobbly fence from 9,000 fans became too great the group fled into cars for the drive to the Hilton Hotel. That night, Billy Preston, who had first met the Beatles in Hamburg in 1962 while playing organ with Ray Charles, visited the group in their 15th-floor suite and took John, Ringo and Neil Aspinall down to the city's Chinatown area. Jet lag obviously wasn't a problem as they didn't return to the hotel until 5.30am.

Wednesday 19th August
The Cow Palace, San Francisco, California

3

The first show of the tour – 17,000 paid £30,000 ($90,000) to see the Beatles play exactly 29 minutes of music, breaking a box-office record previously held by Chubby Checker.

Set-list for the American and Canadian dates (with a few slight amendments) was: 'Twist And Shout', 'You Can't Do That', 'All My Loving', 'She Loves You', 'Things We Said Today', 'Roll Over Beethoven', 'Can't Buy Me Love', 'If I Fell', I Want To Hold Your Hand', 'Boys', 'A Hard Day's Night' and 'Long Tall Sally'.

Support acts on the tour were the Bill Black Combo, the Exciters, the Righteous Brothers and Jackie de Shannon. Backstage, just before the concert, the Beatles met Shirley Temple Black and her 8-year-old daughter, Lori.

"*Although it was publicized as music, all that was heard and seen of the Mersey Sound was something like a jet engine shrieking through a summer lightning storm because of the yelling fans. It had no mercy, and afterward everyone still capable of speech took note of a ringing in the ears which lasted for as long as the Beatles had played*" (from San Francisco Examiner review, 20/8/64).

The Beatles with Shirley Temple and daughter.

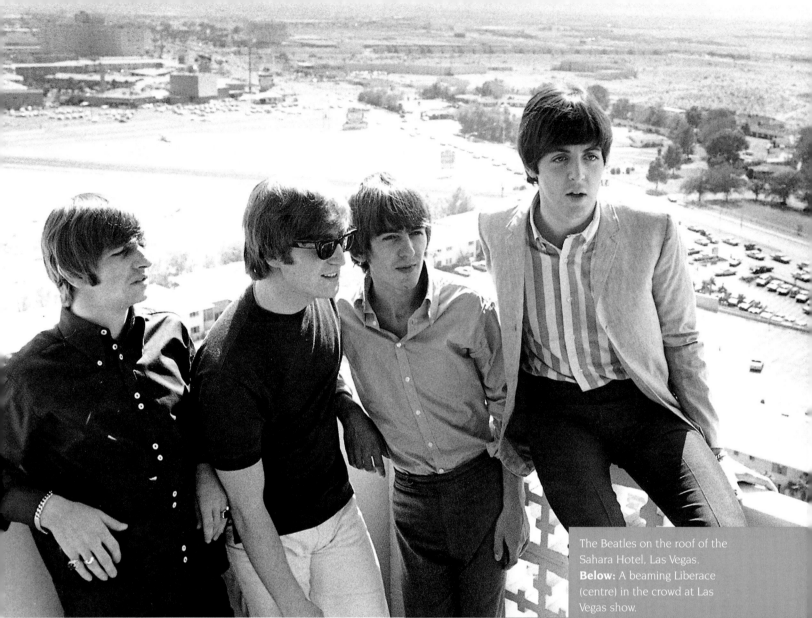

The Beatles on the roof of the Sahara Hotel, Las Vegas.
Below: A beaming Liberace (centre) in the crowd at Las Vegas show.

Thursday 20th August
Convention Center, Las Vegas, Nevada

At just after 1am, the Beatles deplaned at a secret rendezvous in the desert near the McCarron Field terminal building with not a fan in sight. However, their hotel was not such a well-kept secret where, despite curfew hours, 2,000 had gathered. The Beatles had to run the gauntlet when entering the freight entrance at the rear of the Sahara Hotel and took the lift to their 18th-floor penthouse. Police deputies called for reinforcements from the Las Vegas police who, with three police dogs, eventually dispersed the shrieking mob.

The Beatles played two shows (4 and 8pm) to a combined crowd of more than 16,000 people who included Pat Boone, Connie Francis and Liberace.

Paul and George onstage in Las Vegas.

Unable to visit a casino, the one-armed bandits were brought to the Beatles hotel suite.
Bottom left: Beatles publicist Derek Taylor digs for coins.
Bottom right: The Beatles pose in a golf kart for a photo session at the Sahara Hotel.

Friday 21st August
Seattle Center Coliseum, Seattle, Washington

3

Straight after the late Las Vegas concert, the Beatles flew on to Seattle, staying at the Edgewater Inn, which was famous for guests on the waterfront hotel's north elevation being able to fish from the windows – something the Beatles took advantage of. For their one sold-out show, before 14,720, the Beatles were escorted down a corridor across 18 feet of open space and onto the open stage by 16 police officers forming a protective wall. This didn't deter a section of the audience charging the human shield to get to the Beatles. For

their exit, police recruited navy volunteers from the audience and formed them in a double chain stretching from the stage exit to the dressing room corridor, again provoking another audience attack. Such was the level of frenzy that the Beatles became trapped in their dressing room for an hour before they could leave in an ambulance. (The limousine waiting to spirit them away had been crushed.)

Upon returning to the hotel, like a scene from A Hard Day's Night, the Beatles dashed from the limousine as it pulled up at the hotel kerb and ran through the coffee shop entrance and up the stairs to the second floor where Burns Detective Agency uniformed men patrolled the corridor.

That afternoon a hotel maid had discovered two 16-year-old girls in a fourth-floor room, hiding under the bed, with another hidden in the closet. The girls had slipped into the room late Thursday night. "Don't print our names," one of the girls pleaded when handed over to security. "Our folks think we're staying with friends."

Saturday 22nd August

3

The Beatles left Seattle-Tacoma Airport on Saturday afternoon for Vancouver, and drove in a procession along fan-packed streets to Empire Stadium, their first open-air venue, where they played to 20,261 people. Thousands of fans charged across the field, and many were crushed against the fence guarding the stage, resulting in casualties requiring first aid.

From Canada, the Beatles flew direct to Los Angeles, arriving at 3.55am. The American Federation of Musicians, which had prevented the group's Carnegie Hall concert in February being recorded, gave permission for the Beatles' show at the Hollywood Bowl on Sunday 23rd August to be recorded by Capitol Records for a possible live album. The tapes were considered technically below standard, mainly due to the lung power of 18,700 fans, and stayed in the vaults until George Martin went through them and prepared selections from this concert (and the two shows the Beatles played at the Bowl on 29th and 30th August 1965) which EMI released in 1977 as *The Beatles At The Hollywood Bowl*.

On the 24th the Beatles and Brian Epstein attended a charity garden party with over 500 guests at the home of Capitol president, Alan Livingston. Adopting a "grin and bear it" policy, the Beatles met various movie stars' children whose parents had paid $25 a ticket to attend. Stars like Dean Martin, Rock Hudson and Edward G. Robinson, and Hollywood gossip columnists like Hedda Hopper stood on chairs as the kids filed past, shaking hands and having their pictures taken with the famous musicians. About $10,000 was raised for the Haemophilia Foundation of Southern California.

The Beatles had two days off on the 24th and 25th in their rented mansion at No. 356 Saint Pierre Road, Bel Air, which was besieged by snooping fans, who caused an estimated $5,000 of residential property damage. Among the ubiquitous Hollywood celebrities who attached themselves to the group was buxom blonde Jayne Mansfield. When she turned up at the Beatles' rented home, John was the only Beatle around. "Is this real?" Jayne said, pulling his hair. "Well, are those real," Lennon replied, quick as a flash, pointing at her famous chest. Mansfield with John, George and Ringo tried to slip unnoticed into the Whisky A Go Go on Sunset Strip until an unwanted photographer Bob Flora got a drink thrown at him by George. With their visit causing chaos, the Beatles party left after 10 minutes, being driven back to Bel Air in a police car.

HOLLYWOOD BOWL
2301 H. Highland Ave.
HOLLYWOOD   CALIFORNIA
AUG.   SUNDAY EVE. 8:00 P.M.
No one seated during performance
23   **THE BEATLES**
           IN CONCERT
1964   ESTAB. PRICE $3.27 **$3.50**
           FEDERAL TAX .23
           NO REFUNDS - NO EXCHANGES

U 2 14
RESERVED
SEC.
ROW
SEAT

GOOD ONLY
SUNDAY EVE.
AUGUST
HOLLYWOOD BOWL
23
1964
RESERVED $3.50

The Beatles meet the children of Hollywood. Mal Evans stands to the right with Neil Aspinall and Brian Epstein (both in shades) behind.

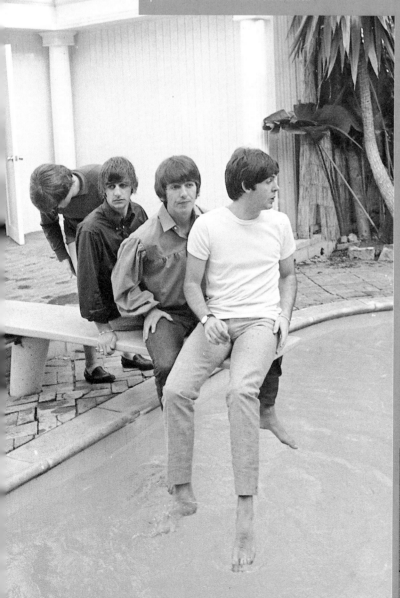

Relaxing at their rented home in Bel Air. Ringo's gun holster was a present from Colonel Tom Parker.

Friday 28th and Saturday 29th August
Forest Hills Tennis Stadium, Forest Hills, New York

The Beatles arrived at Kennedy International Airport from Cincinnati at 2.55am on Friday the 28th. A crowd of 3,000 who had waited for up to 24 hours to see them only got a brief glimpse as airport officials swept the group away into a limo in two minutes flat. Across from the Delmonico Hotel on Park Avenue, crowds of up to 3,000 kept a day and night vigil behind police barriers and screamed as long-haired figures appeared for a second at windows, but it turned out to be ordinary guests wearing Beatle wigs.

Like other stops on the tour, the originally booked hotel, the Lincoln Center Motor Inn, refused to accept the Beatles' reservations for fear of fan activity. But as a Delmonico spokesman said, "We welcome the Beatles. We used to be dowdy, but now we swing!"

Police would not accept responsibility for the Beatles' safety if they travelled to Queens by car so a helicopter was arranged to ferry them there and back. At the Friday show, where the Beatles were an hour late, dozens of fans stormed the stage. Despite 300 police and 200 Burns Agency guards hired to keep the crowd of 16,000 under control, four girls evaded security guarding the front of the stage and Ringo was knocked from his drum stool. "I couldn't stop laughing," John said afterwards. "They were all jumping on stage and the cops were fighting 'em off as we played. There must have been 15 cops on stage with us when we sang 'She Loves You'. There've never been so many Beatles."

"They [the Beatles] have created a monster in their audience. If they have concern for anything, they had better concern themselves with controlling their audiences before this contrived hysteria reaches uncontrollable proportions." (The New York Times, 30/8/ 64).

During one of the group's nights off, in their sixth-floor suite at the Delmonico, journalist Al Aronowitz brought the Beatles and Bob Dylan together for the first time. (The Beatles had first heard the folk poet while in Paris earlier in the year.) Dylan had thought to bring some marijuana with him as he misheard the repeated "I can't hide" line in 'I Want To Hold Your Hand' as "I get high". Like amphetamines in Hamburg, pot had an immediate effect on the Beatles, acting as a relaxant while opening up new vistas for John and Paul's song-writing. Dylan would also act as an influence – most notably in the Lennon songs 'I'm A Loser' and 'You've Got To Hide Your Love Away'.

John gets caught in a tussle as the Beatles arrive at Forest Hills.

George in Atlantic City with Neil Aspinall, who is holding the programme for the US tour.

George playing monopoly with tour support artist Jackie de Shannon.

The Beatles spent most of their three days at this coastal resort, imprisoned at the Lafayette Motor Inn. While George whiled away the hours playing Monopoly with tour support Jackie de Shannon, Paul chatted to his idol, Elvis Presley, in a phone call arranged by British journalist Chris Hutchins (or Crisp Hutchy as the Beatles called him) who was covering the tour for the *New Musical Express*. Paul and John also wrote 'Every Little Thing' and 'What You're Doing' (both on *Beatles For Sale*) during the break.

Until a stretch of barbed wire was strung along the wall surrounding the motel, fans had tried climbing in and had used empty soda bottles to fill water from the pool in which the Beatles had taken a private dip and were selling it for $1 a bottle!

Ringo was undoubtedly the most popular Beatle in America in 1964. Having spent the first 18 months of his time in the Beatles as the self-conscious "new boy" hovering in the background, this newfound image as the sad clown, fostered by his character in *A Hard Day's Night*, had boosted his status.

Wednesday 2nd September
Convention Hall, Philadelphia, Pennsylvania

At 2.15pm the Beatles were smuggled out of the Lafayette Motor Inn, sitting in the back of a fish truck, and driven six miles west of Atlantic City, where they transferred to a 60-seater coach which drove unnoticed into the Convention Hall.

The extensive North American tour continued in whirlwind fashion with the customary airport-car-hotel room-car-press conference-dressing room-concert-car-hotel room-car-airport cycle repeated ad infinitum. But the mania from fans, the press and overzealous police officials was taking its mental and physical toll. As George later remarked, "People used the Beatles as an excuse to go mad. Even the cops were out of line. 'Oh, and here come the

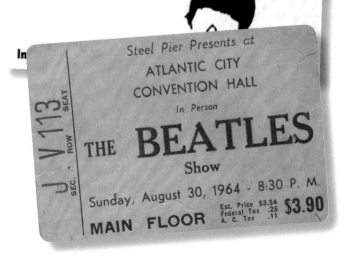

Beatles, let's all get crazy and rip up limousines' and we were in the middle of it all, getting the blame."

In Indianapolis there was a telephoned threat that the Beatles would be injured by either "a gun or an explosion", and in Montreal Ringo spent the whole gig playing while ducking low below his cymbals, after a reported death threat. During the tour, a popular psychic, Jeane Dixon, who allegedly had predicted Kennedy's assassination, forecast that three Beatles would be killed when their chartered Lockheed Electra would crash in Indiana. (While this, thankfully, did not occur the same plane did crash two years later killing all on board.)

Arriving in Jacksonville, the plane was buffeted by winds left over from Hurricane Dora. In Cleveland, the show was stopped for 10 minutes by police anxieties over rioting fans. Police Inspector Michael Blackwell ordered the group from the stage, physically manhandling George by his elbow towards the wings. If all this wasn't enough, at some shows, disabled children were brought before the Beatles as if their magnetism extended to Messianic faith healing. Understandably, the Beatles were horrified by the sight and a cry of "Cripples, Nel" from a Beatle was a code for Neil Aspinall to clear the dressing room of any unwanted visitors.

Thanks to their now all-enveloping fame the Beatles were considered a hot business proposition for various entrepreneurs. Instead of a scheduled day off, the group were paid a record fee of £53,000 ($150,000) by local promoter Charles O. Finley to play an extra show at Kansas City's Municipal Stadium on 17th September. However, Finley failed to profit from the venture as only 20,000 of a possible 41,000 attended, with 28,000 needed to break even. Another to lose out was Chicago businessman Lawrence Einhorn who bought the rumpled bed linen the Beatles used during their stay at the Muehlebach Towers Hotel in Kansas City for $750. Einhorn cut the material into squares to sell as merchandise but there weren't as many takers as he'd hoped.

The merchandizing side – something that was largely unchartered territory in pop music – provided an absolute boon for an American company called Seltaeb (Beatles spelt backwards) which profited hugely after being given a large majority company share of 90 per cent – reduced after renegotiations to 54 per cent in August '64 once a horrified Brian Epstein realized the extent of the business gaffe. Epstein had only considered the revenue from the sale of Beatles novelty products (e.g. T-shirts, wigs, badges, talcum powder, plates, etc.) as simply extra gravy that supplemented the Beatles' income from record sales and live shows. It was to be a costly misjudgement.

The Beatles arrive home from America with Brian Epstein and Derek Taylor behind.

Monday 21st September

The Beatles touched down at London Airport at 9.35pm on Flight number BA510, to be greeted by 8,000 fans on the roof of the Queen's Building. Beatles' records were played through the airport's PA system for two hours before the group's arrival, interspersed with regular updates on the flight's progress. The airport authorities decided not to allow the Beatles' customary airport press and TV conference for "safety reasons".

The Beatles' 1964 American tour had cash advances larger than any in entertainment history and reportedly grossed $2,112,000. An Anglo-American tax treaty stated that the Beatles' earnings were liable to British tax. However, US authorities obtained a court order freezing $1,000,000 in proceeds until clarification could be sought. When the dust settled the Beatles reportedly made £360,000 from the tour.

Friday 9th October
Gaumont Theatre, Bradford, Yorkshire

The Beatles had barely three weeks' rest from their exhausting American trek before the opening shows on an autumn British tour, comprising two houses over 27 dates, earning them an impressive £850 per night. Support acts were the Rustiks, Michael Haslam, Sounds Incorporated, the Remo Four, Tommy Quickly and American Motown singer (and Beatles favourite), Mary Wells.

Set-list (for the tour): 'Twist And Shout', 'Money', 'Can't Buy Me Love', 'Things We Said Today', 'I'm Happy Just To Dance With You', 'I Should Have Known Better', 'If I Fell', 'I Wanna Be Your Man', 'A Hard Day's Night', 'Long Tall Sally' and an instrumental of 'Twist And Shout' as the curtain closed.

On John's 24th birthday the Beatles were chauffeur-driven up to Bradford in their Austin Princess but were two hours late in arriving. "Don't blame us," said Paul. "There were traffic jams as we drove up from London. We were worried when a police car flagged us down on the M1, but they only wanted our autographs."

The press reported on the "rows of empty seats" at the first house which was put down to exorbitant ticket prices ranging from 12s 6d for the balcony to 17s 9d for the best seats in the front stalls. Also, so-called "deadly rivals" the Rolling Stones had appeared at the same venue just 14 days earlier. Joint promoters Arthur Howes and Brian Epstein explained away the empty seats as a "muddle over reservations". Said Brian: "We could have sold out the theatre two or three times over. I blame bad handling and management."

John holding five-year-old fan Karen Spence, who presented him with a birthday card for his 24th birthday. She was supposed to sing 'Happy Birthday' too but was put off by all the cameras.

The Beatles with US Motown singer Mary Wells.

Actor Richard Harris (who had recently been acclaimed for his role in the 1963 classic *This Sporting Life*) and his wife Elizabeth Rees-Williams called backstage between shows but found the Beatles unreceptive to visitors. John, apparently suffering from toothache, wrapped himself in a green plastic mac and lay down behind a sofa, while George pretended to be asleep. It was left to the more hospitable Paul and Ringo to look after the visiting VIPs. (At the Beatles' insistence, dressing room access to press, fans and officialdom was significantly reduced.)

At the end of the late show, a decoy was arranged at the main exit while the Beatles ran out a side door and into their car which drove out of Bradford along Thornton Road towards Queensbury, followed by fans and the media in cars as far as The Raggles Inn where the police had formed a roadblock that stopped every car after the Beatles sped through to their pre-booked overnight stay at the Cavalier Country Club in Holmfield near Halifax.

Above and overleaf: The Beatles backstage at the De Montfort Hall, Leicester.

These fan scenes at Leicester show how Beatlemania had hardly abated a year on.

Ringo and John lead the way from Stephenson Place, through a cellar in order to get safely to the Birmingham Odeon, 11th October.

Saturday 10th October
De Montfort Hall, Leicester

After lunch at a hotel near Nottingham the Beatles drove to Leicester and into the police station to await an escort to the De Montfort Hall. Ringo spent time before the first house looking at cars (he had passed his driving test on 8th October). During one of the shows, a fan threw onstage a large Gonk (a doll that was popular in the mid-Sixties), which John picked up and placed on his amp. Instead of staying overnight, the group were driven back to London before the next night's shows in Birmingham.

Thursday 15th October
Globe Cinema, Stockton-on-Tees

The 1964 General Election occurred while the Beatles were on tour, with Harold Wilson's Labour government winning by a narrow margin over the Tories. On Election Day (15th October), when they were appearing in Stockton, the Beatles were too busy to vote, with a "disappointed" Paul explaining to the Northern edition of the *Mirror*, "We didn't get our voting papers in time. We wanted to have postal votes, but our forms were sent off too late. That means we can't vote today, unless we go back to our own constituencies in Liverpool."

At their hotel, an ITN *reporter interrupted the Beatles' tea break.*

Reporter: *You're regular top of the pollsters, what do you think about this election business?*

Ringo: *It's alright if you win.*

Reporter: *What do you think is going to happen if they have to nationalize you?*

George: *Well, we'll have to move out, won't we? We'd have to go and live in Germany or someplace like that.*

John: *Southern Ireland's only half an hour away.*

Reporter: *Did you have time to vote yourselves?*

John (pointedly): *We were having dinner at the time…*

During the last few weeks, the Grimond group, the Home group and the Wilson group have been edging you off the papers. Have you been envious of them?

Paul: *No, we sell more records.*

John: *Just don't take our money, Harold!*

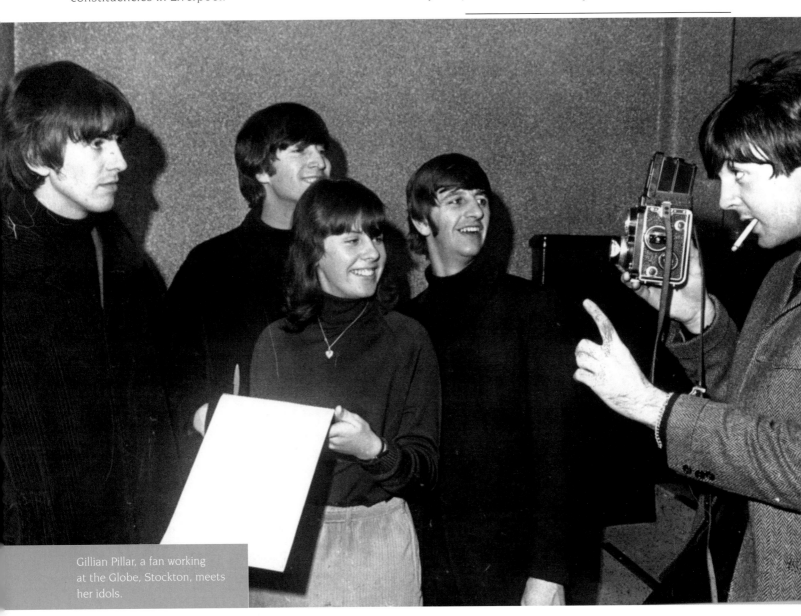

Gillian Pillar, a fan working at the Globe, Stockton, meets her idols.

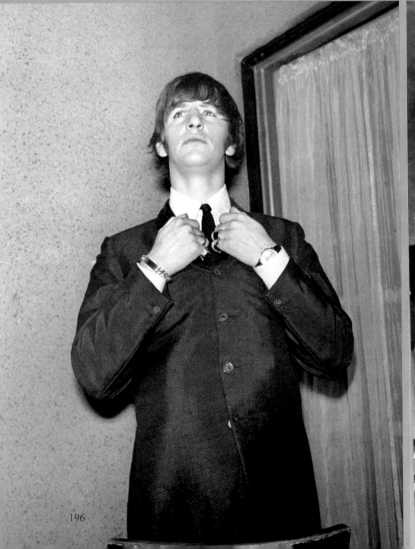

196

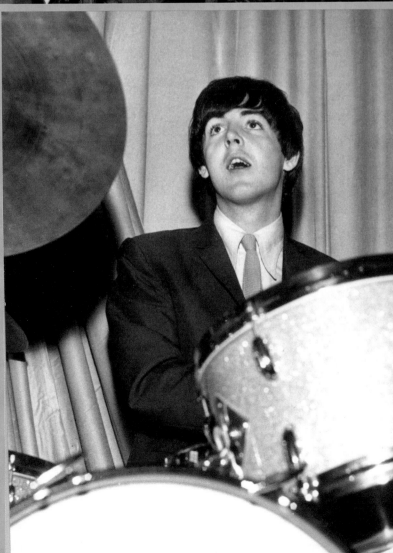

Monday 19th October
ABC Cinema, Edinburgh

The Beatles' third Scottish visit in a year and, despite certain naysayers, was just as frenzied as ever with sold-out shows in Edinburgh, Dundee and Glasgow. Outside the Glasgow Odeon (on 21st October), fans took out their frustration at not being able to get inside the theatre to see the group by smashing shop windows in Renfrew Street, and when the crowd was corralled into West George Street by mounted police, a parked car was overturned, spilling out petrol which was hurriedly doused by firemen before disaster struck.

"Beatles bombarded with jelly babies."

"Fantastic scenes greeted the appearance of the Beatles at Edinburgh's ABC Theatre last night ...

"The theatre erupted when the Fab Four made their appearance and all through their act they ran the gauntlet of a hail of jelly babies. The boys stormed through 10 numbers unheard by the hysterical audience.

"The evening was trouble free although the Red Cross ran a shuttle service for overexcited fans, who took no further part in the proceedings.

"At the end of the first house, excited fans roamed around the theatre chanting pro-Beatles slogans.

"The supporting bill was a mixture of good and bad, and only Sounds Incorporated made any real impression with their powerful, well-drilled act. American vocalist, Mary Wells presented an act more suited to the intimate atmosphere of a nightclub. The Beatles themselves were in tip-top form, and Dundee fans are certainly guaranteed a treat tonight."

(Dundee Courier And Advertiser, 20/10/64).

Tuesday 20th October

Seconds after the curtain fell at the end of their second appearance in the packed Edinburgh ABC in Lothian Road, the Beatles dashed out of the theatre and sped off in two waiting cars which passed over the new Forth Road Bridge on the 65-mile drive to the Four Seasons Hotel, in St Fillans, at the east end of Loch Earn. The Beatles slept late and rose to a typical breakfast of orange juice, cornflakes and tea. The location of their hideaway hotel remained a secret and even the teenagers in the quiet little village were initially unaware that the famous foursome were in their midst.

Helping themselves to ice at a press reception at the Odeon, Leeds, 22nd October.

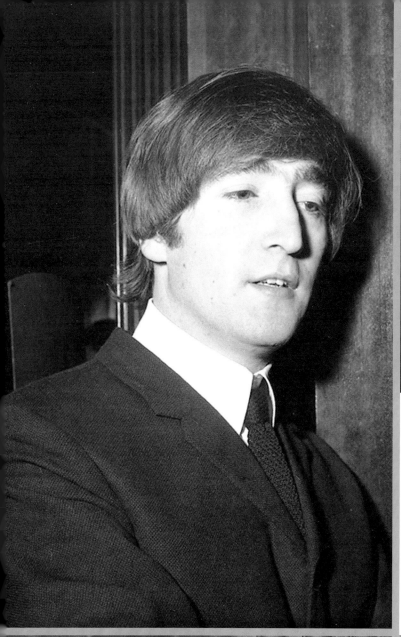

Friday 23rd October
Gaumont State, Kilburn, London

3

The Beatles were originally pencilled in to play the Rank Organization's New Victoria Theatre in London on this date.

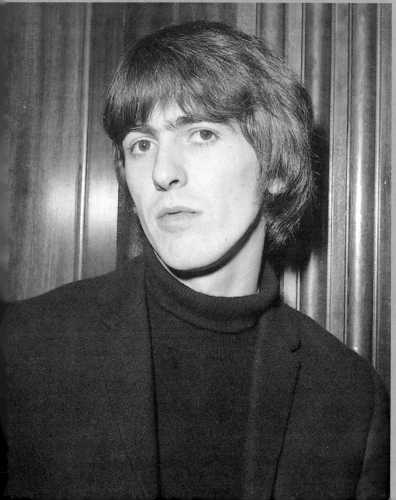

The Beatles at press reception
at the Kilburn Gaumont.

Below: Paul and Ringo with toy gun and plastic Beatles guitar backstage in Belfast. They presented the items to local volunteers in a toys-for-Christmas campaign for the city's orphans.

Monday 2nd November
King's Hall, Belfast, Northern Ireland

For what was originally a free day in the Beatles' schedule, it was decided to fit in a quick visit to Ireland as England, Scotland and Wales had been represented. The gig also offered a convenient escape clause as the Beatles had been invited to make a return appearance to the Royal Variety Show, held that year at the Palladium. Already showing no desire to repeat themselves, the request was politely turned down – as it would be again the following year. Paul explained, "Over 4,000 tickets had been sold for the Belfast show and we couldn't let the Belfast kids down."

"There was never any intention of snubbing the Queen of course," John hurriedly added. The King's Hall concert, which attracted around 17,500, turned out to be the Beatles' largest gig ever in the United Kingdom.

Ringo makes a lewd gesture at Liverpool Empire press conference.

Sunday 8th November
Empire Theatre, Liverpool

The Beatles' first concerts in their hometown in almost a year.

Without any incidents to report, the *Mirror*'s Northern edition quoted Chief Constable Joseph Smith as telling the group, "I want to thank you for all you've done for the city. You're a great bunch of guys."

The British tour ended two nights later in Bristol. Apart from some TV and radio plugs for their new single and album, the Beatles had a much-needed six weeks off.

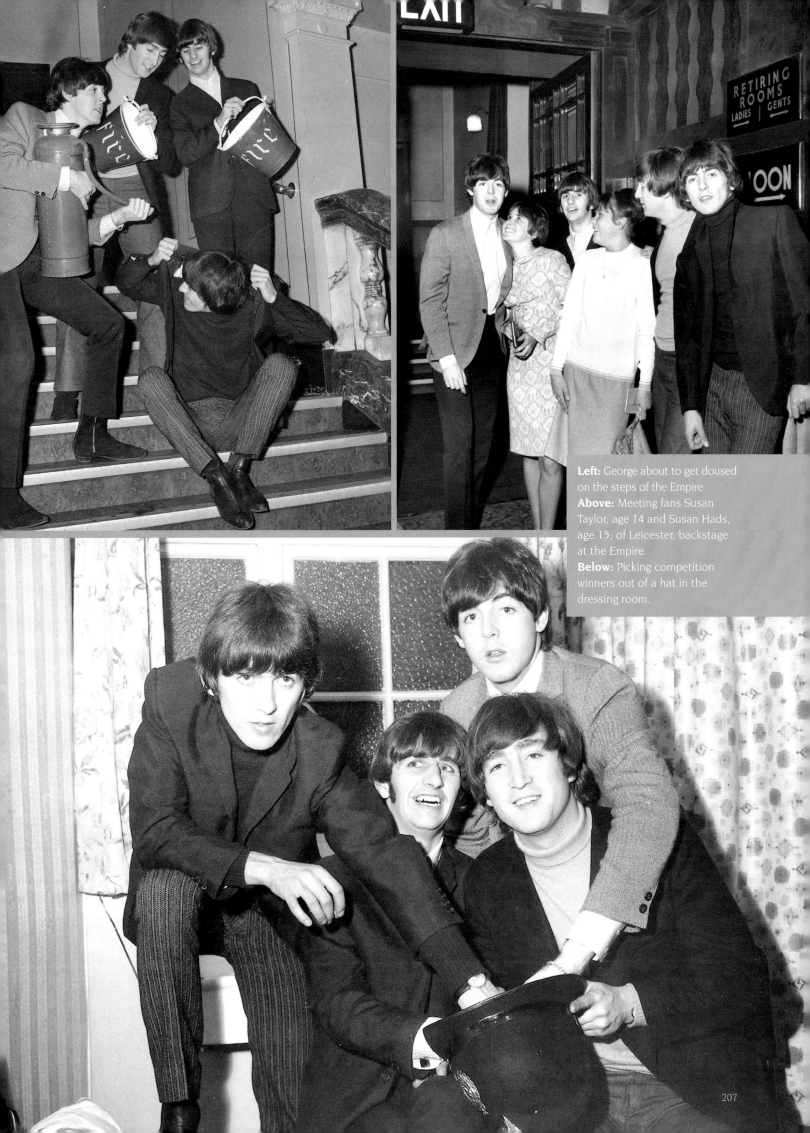

Left: George about to get doused on the steps of the Empire
Above: Meeting fans Susan Taylor, age 14 and Susan Hads, age 15, of Leicester, backstage at the Empire.
Below: Picking competition winners out of a hat in the dressing room.

Thursday 24th December – Thursday 31st December

"Another Beatles Christmas Show", Odeon Theatre, Hammersmith, London

The show was announced back in early June and tickets for the three-week run at the Rank Organization's largest theatre (now the HMV Hammersmith Apollo), which seated up to 3,500, went on sale on Monday 7th September. Despite there being 150,000 tickets available, fans started gathering at 11pm the previous evening, and by the following morning a 500-yard queue had formed.

Artists appearing on the bill were (in order): the Mike Cotton Sound, Michael Haslam, the Yardbirds and Freddie and The Dreamers (closing the first half), with Elkie Brooks, Sounds Incorporated and the Beatles. Compere: Jimmy Savile.

Like the previous year's presentation at the Finsbury Park Astoria, the show was produced by Peter Yolland, who was also committed to staging Gerry's Christmas Cracker, a similar family-styled pantomime starring Gerry and The Pacemakers, in Liverpool, Leeds and Glasgow.

The Beatles turned up at the Odeon for rehearsals on Monday 21st December. Their 30-minute set consisted of: 'Twist And Shout', 'She's A Woman', 'I'm A Loser', 'Everybody's Trying To Be My Baby', 'Baby's In Black', 'Honey Don't', 'A Hard Day's Night', 'I Feel Fine' and 'Long Tall Sally'.

Like the previous year, Yolland wrote several comedy sketches featuring the Beatles, who were reportedly unhappy at having to participate in what were admittedly weak spots – one featuring them dressed up as polar explorers in search of Jimmy Savile as the Abominable Snowman, another depicting them as waxworks dummies. It was the last presentation of its kind to feature the Beatles in this way.

The Beatles with Jimmy Savile and Freddie Garrity.

Dressed as Eskimos at
Hammersmith Odeon
press launch.
Top left: The Beatles and
Christmas Show cast.
Far left: John Lennon's drawing
adorns the cover of programme.

Ticket To Ride

"One has to completely humiliate oneself to be what the Beatles were... it just happened bit by bit until this complete craziness is surrounding you, and you're doing exactly what you don't want to do with people you can't stand — the people you hated when you were ten."

John Lennon, *Rolling Stone*, 1970

1965

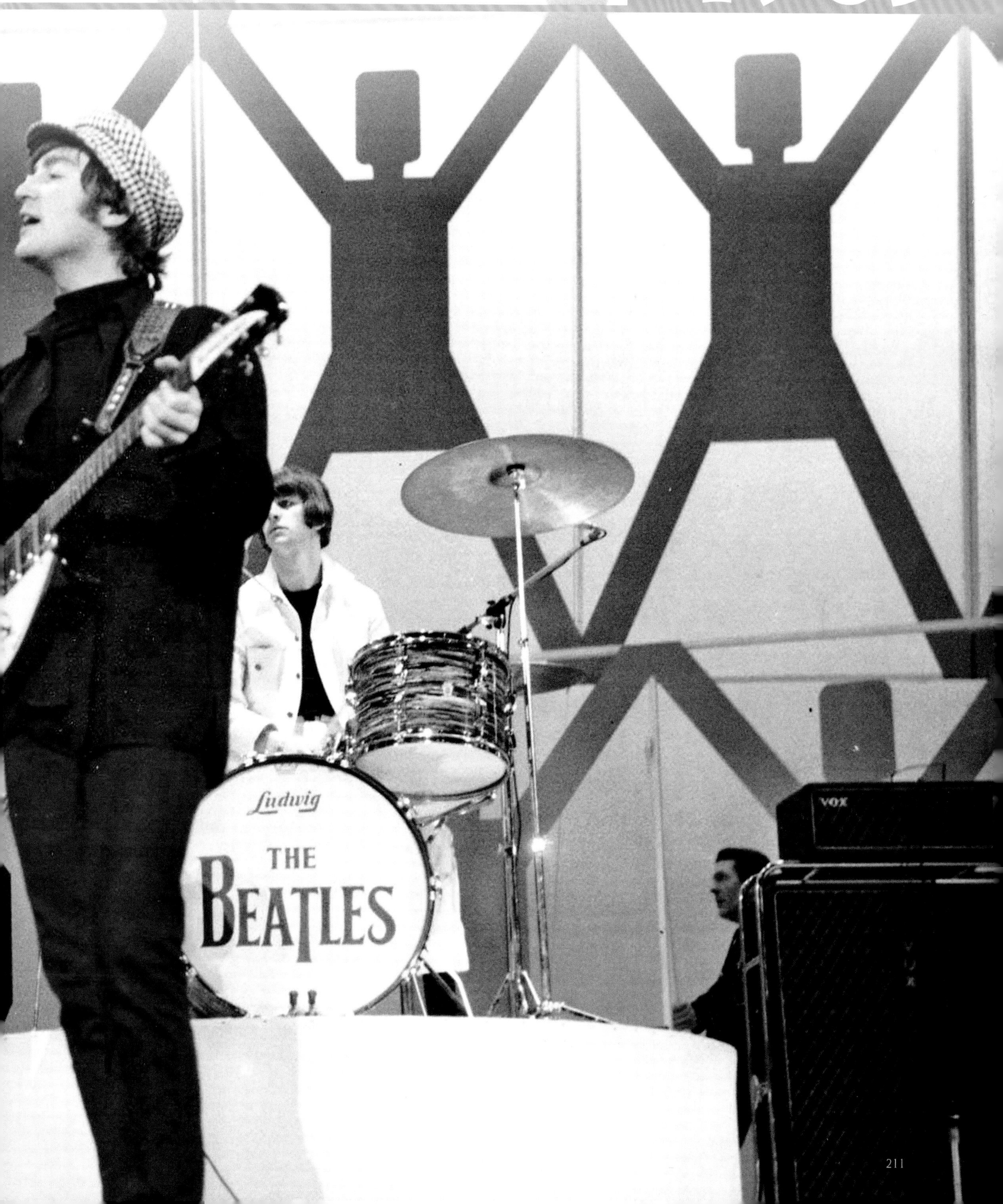

For two years, the relentless pace of the Beatles' lives – both in the public eye and behind the scenes – had left them with little time to take stock. However, the sheer intensity of 1964 could not have continued and the seemingly out-of-control madness of Beatlemania was finally brought to something approaching order in 1965. Apart from a not entirely successful summer European tour that was undertaken largely at the behest of EMI to increase the Beatles' saleability in France, Italy and Spain, for the first half of the year the Beatles played no other concert dates except for a perfunctory appearance at the annual NME Poll Winners Concert at the Empire Pool, Wembley on 11th April. In August the Beatles returned to America for the third time, pioneering shows at large outdoor venues where maximum revenue could be generated to meet the demand. Nowhere was this better demonstrated than their record-breaking show at New York's Shea Stadium on 15th August before an audience of 56,000.

With the Beatles' worldwide popularity now established, the Mirror felt less inclined to cover the group's overseas exploits in such depth, apart from the inevitable fan gatherings at Heathrow Airport whenever the Beatles flew out for – and back from – their latest overseas jaunt.

The year's headlines were mainly dominated by events off the stage: Ringo's wedding to Maureen Cox on 11th February and the birth of their first son Zak in September; the Beatles making their second film Help! in colour and with a bigger budget on location in the Bahamas, the Austrian Alps, the Salisbury Plain and at Twickenham Film Studios; John's second book A Spaniard In The Works and, most notably, being honoured by Harold Wilson's Labour government as Members of the Most Excellent Order of the British Empire in the Queen's Birthday Honours list, justified by their contribution to the Balance of Payments, and the resulting furore involving returned medals from decorated holders.

In between, the Beatles slotted in interviews and photo sessions, television and radio appearances (although these were far fewer than the previous year) as well as studio sessions at EMI which were still strictly controlled affairs with morning, afternoon and evening session times being adhered to. It wasn't until recording commenced in October for the landmark Rubber Soul album that the Beatles started to dictate their own terms with the first of many all-night recording sessions. With John and Paul's song-writing continuing to mature and George also starting to blossom as a writer – thanks to the wealth of their shared experiences and the outside influence of drugs – greater time was needed in the studio. As their creativity increased so did their antipathy towards touring – being shunted in and out of airports (none of the group liked flying), hotels and venues to the never-ending background of screaming crowds who couldn't hear the music.

Significantly, the issue of the New Musical Express (the British weekly music paper that tended to be the first to break Beatles stories), dated 6th August, reported that the Beatles would definitely not tour Britain that year. However, three weeks later, the paper did an about turn saying that the Beatles might undertake a British tour in 1965 after all. An invitation to reappear in that year's Royal Variety Show and plans for a third Christmas Show were vetoed outright, as was a performance to be transmitted to cinemas via closed-circuit TV. One can only imagine the amount of persuasion Brian Epstein had to employ to cajole the Beatles into dragging themselves on a short haul around Britain's Odeons and ABCs at the end of the year. As the Beatles' public image was subtly changing, the weariness and fatigue that surfaced during tours was now harder to disguise and the appeal of playing live had definitely worn away. The following year was to prove a turning point.

THE BEATLES

HELP!

SEVEN NEW SONGS

LEO McKERN   ELEANOR BRON   VICTOR SPINETTI   ROY KINNEAR   EASTMAN COLOUR

produced by WALTER SHENSON screenplay by MARC BEHM & CHARLES WOOD story by MARC BEHM directed by RICHARD LESTER

ROYAL WORLD PREMIERE
in the gracious presence of HER ROYAL HIGHNESS THE PRINCESS MARGARET, COUNTESS OF SNOWDON and the EARL OF SNOWDON
Sponsored by the Variety Club of Great Britain
in aid of THE DOCKLAND SETTLEMENTS SCHOOL OF ADVENTURE and THE VARIETY CLUB HEART FUND
at the
LONDON PAVILION
PICCADILLY CIRCUS
on
THURSDAY JULY 29th 1965

GENERAL RELEASE FROM AUG. 1

Sunday 11th April

New Musical Express Poll Winners Concert, Empire Pool, Wembley

A return to the annual event, where the Beatles scooped Top British Vocal Group and Top World Vocal Group awards in the 1964/65 poll, presented by American crooner Tony Bennett. John was also awarded runner-up in the British Vocal Personality section.

Keith Fordyce introduced the Beatles with, "There are many, many million words in the English language, many of these words are adjectives but I'm not going to use any of them, they've been done to death by critics and comperes alike and there aren't any [words] left for these artists... let's just have it completely silent for one second while I say... The Beatles."

The group took to the stage in their new stage uniforms of khaki-coloured jackets and black polo necks with black trousers.

Set-list: 'I Feel Fine' (featuring John playing his Gibson Jumbo acoustic which was responsible for the feedback at the start of the song), 'She's A Woman', 'Baby's In Black', 'Ticket To Ride' (which had just been released as the Beatles' latest single – and eighth No. 1), and 'Long Tall Sally'.

John and Ringo nonchalantly chewed gum throughout the performance – something that would have been unthinkable three years earlier when Brian Epstein insisted on cleaning up the Beatles' act – and considering the NME concert was to be televised, it showed who was increasingly calling the shots.

MAURICE KINN
presents the

new

MUSICAL EXPRESS

1964-65 ANNUAL
POLL-WINNERS ALL-STAR CONCERT

SUNDAY, APRIL 11th, 1965
EMPIRE POOL, WEMBLEY

OFFICIAL PROGRAMME   PRICE **1/6**

20 Pages

THE EMPIRE POOL AND SPORTS ARENA, WEMBLEY

APRIL 11

ADMIT AT— SOUTH DOOR

MAURICE KINN presents the ANNUAL
"NEW MUSICAL EXPRESS"
POLL WINNERS CONCERT

SUNDAY, APRIL 11th, 1965
at 2 p.m.   Doors open 1.30 p.m.

BLOCK C

RESERVED SEAT

30/-

ROW 13
SEAT 31

CONDITION   Neither Wembley Stadium Limited nor the Concert Promoters shall be under any legal liability for any injury loss or damage sustained by the ticket holder howsoever caused and admittance is at holder's sole risk.

TO BE RETAINED

216

Sunday 20th June

4

The Beatles took a morning flight from London to Paris – a subdued farewell as airport authorities had forbade fans from assembling – relaxing at the Hotel George V before travelling on to the Palais des Sport for the first concerts (3 and 9pm) of a two-week European tour.

Tour set-list: 'Twist And Shout', 'She's A Woman', 'I'm A Loser', 'Can't Buy Me Love', 'Baby's In Black', 'I Wanna Be Your Man', 'A Hard Day's Night', 'Everybody's Trying To Be My Baby', 'Rock And Roll Music', 'I Feel Fine', 'Ticket To Ride', and encore 'Long Tall Sally'.

Both shows before a total audience of 6,000 – again, as with their January '64 visit, mainly male – were recorded and broadcast, while the evening show was also filmed. Afterwards the whole Beatle entourage went on to the Castelles Club to unwind.

The Beatles' European tour itinerary took in Lyon, Milan, Genoa, Rome (where the Beatles went sightseeing unmolested in the early hours of Monday 28th June), Nice, Madrid and Barcelona, returning to London Airport on Sunday 4th July at 12 noon.

Opposite and preceding pages: The Beatles onstage in Paris, 20th June.
Below: On hotel balcony in Nice, 29th June.

217

Above and preceding pages:
Rehearsing at the ABC Theatre,
Blackpool.

Sunday 1ˢᵗ August
ABC Theatre, Blackpool

The day that the film *Help!* went on general release around Britain, the Beatles made a special live appearance on Mike and Bernie Winters' annual summer showcase *Blackpool Night Out*, broadcast between 9.10 and 10.05pm. Significantly, it was to be the group's only personal television appearance to plug their latest single, 'Help!', released 23ʳᵈ July.

While Ringo flew up to Blackpool with Brian Epstein, John, Paul and George took John's black Rolls-Royce up for the journey. Performing live had necessitated some rehearsal for the new songs and the Beatles spent time in London at the Saville Theatre (recently leased by Brian Epstein) on Shaftesbury Avenue. They also had lengthy conferrals with the sound technicians at the ABC Theatre after their previous live appearance on the programme (19ᵗʰ July 1964) had been blighted by poor sound balance. "We can understand the problem," Paul told the NME. "After each number they only have about two seconds to get it right. In a recording studio you spend two hours doing the same thing."
Songs performed: 'I Feel Fine', 'I'm Down' (with John on electric Vox organ), 'Act Naturally', 'Ticket To Ride', 'Yesterday' (performed live for the first time by Paul solo on acoustic backed by the house orchestra) and 'Help!'.

Paul rehearses 'Yesterday' for the song's first-ever live airing.

CBS TELEVISION NETWORK
TELEVISION STUDIO NO. 50
1697 BROADWAY, AT 53 ST., N.Y.C.

AUG. 14, 7 PM   COMPLIMENTARY—NOT FOR SALE
LEVER BROS.   KENT CIGARETTES
BURLINGTON INDUSTRIES, Inc.

Present
THE ED SULLIVAN SHOW
Taping—For Future Broadcast   See Other Side

STUDIO NO. 50
7—8 PM
DOORS OPEN 6:15 PM
DOORS CLOSE 6:45 PM

639

CBS

GOOD ONLY
SAT. EVE.
AUGUST

1965   14

Friday 13th August

Despite the superstitious date, the Beatles flew from London Airport at noon to New York to commence their third American tour, arriving at 2.30pm local time in a remote area of JFK Airport away from fans.

While in the Big Apple, as well as taping an *Ed Sullivan Show* appearance (where they performed the same set as in Blackpool) for later broadcast on Sunday 12th September, the undoubted highlight – and the absolute pinnacle of the

Beatles' concert career – was their record-breaking concert at Shea Stadium, home of the New York Mets baseball team, in Queens on 15th August, before 55,600 – with a gross of $304,000 – a showbiz record for the time. The Beatles performed 12 songs in just 30 minutes.

Set-list (and for the tour): 'Twist And Shout', 'She's A Woman', 'I Feel Fine', 'Dizzy Miss Lizzy', 'Ticket To Ride', 'Everybody's Trying To Be My Baby', 'Can't Buy Me Love', 'Baby's In Black', 'I Wanna Be Your Man', 'A Hard Day's Night', 'Help!' and 'I'm Down'.

Tour support acts were the King Curtis Band, Cannibal and the Headhunters, Brenda Holloway and Sounds Incorporated.

Thursday 2nd September

The Beatles touched down at London Airport just before 7am to be met by a gaggle of fans, an unexpected surprise considering the early hour. As John remarked, "They should all be given the MBE".

The Beatles' American tour grossed £357,000. With no other commitments on their severely reduced schedule they enjoyed almost six weeks off.

At the Glasgow press conference John pretends to blow his nose on Paul's new kipper tie bought from Harrods.

Friday 3rd December
Odeon Theatre, Glasgow

The Beatles' final British tour, performing 18 concerts in eight different cities, began north of the border. Tickets for the concerts had gone on sale on Sunday 31st October and demand was still high; for the Liverpool concerts, 40,000 ticket applications were received for a venue that held only 2,550. The same day that the tour opened, the Beatles' newest single, a double A-side of 'Day Tripper'/ 'We Can Work It Out' and album,

Rubber Soul, were released as Christmas stocking fillers, both claiming respective top spots over the Yuletide period.

Set-list: 'I Feel Fine', 'She's A Woman', 'If I Needed Someone', 'Act Naturally', 'Nowhere Man', 'Baby's In Black', 'Help!', 'We Can Work It Out' (with John on Vox organ), 'Yesterday' (with Paul accompanying himself on organ), 'Day Tripper' and 'I'm Down' (with John on organ).

The Beatles had left London early on Thursday 2nd December and stayed overnight in the border town of Berwick-upon-Tweed. During the drive into Scotland, George's Gretsch Country Gentleman, worth £300, which, along with some other equipment, had been fastened to the boot of the group's Austin Princess by driver Alf Bicknell, fell off and was crushed to pieces by heavy traffic following behind.

Alf Bicknell: "*The driver of this great big articulated lorry signalled for me to pull over. He said to me, 'I think you've dropped a banjo back down the road.' So I went and looked at the back of the car and sure enough, one of the guitars was missing. I thought that's my lot. I said to Neil [Aspinall], 'You'd better tell them what's happened.' He said, 'No you tell 'em.' So I put my head into the car and said, 'I think we've lost a guitar'. There was a pause and out of the darkness John said, 'Well if you find it, you'll get a bonus.' I was always a little wary of John so I said, 'What's the bonus?' He said, 'You can have your job back!'*"

The police had insisted that the streets around the Odeon were sealed off (as they would be at the following shows in Newcastle and Liverpool), resulting in the theatre being virtually deserted out front. Only ticket holders were allowed through and even then they were ordered to make their way directly inside.

"It's always the same at the start of a tour," John Lennon told Alan Walsh of *Melody Maker*. "We've done it hundreds of times but we are always nervous just the same. It's funny because, once we're on stage, it all goes. It will be the same at Liverpool on Sunday. Liverpool's home, and they all know us, and we're sort of expected to do well and we get nervous."

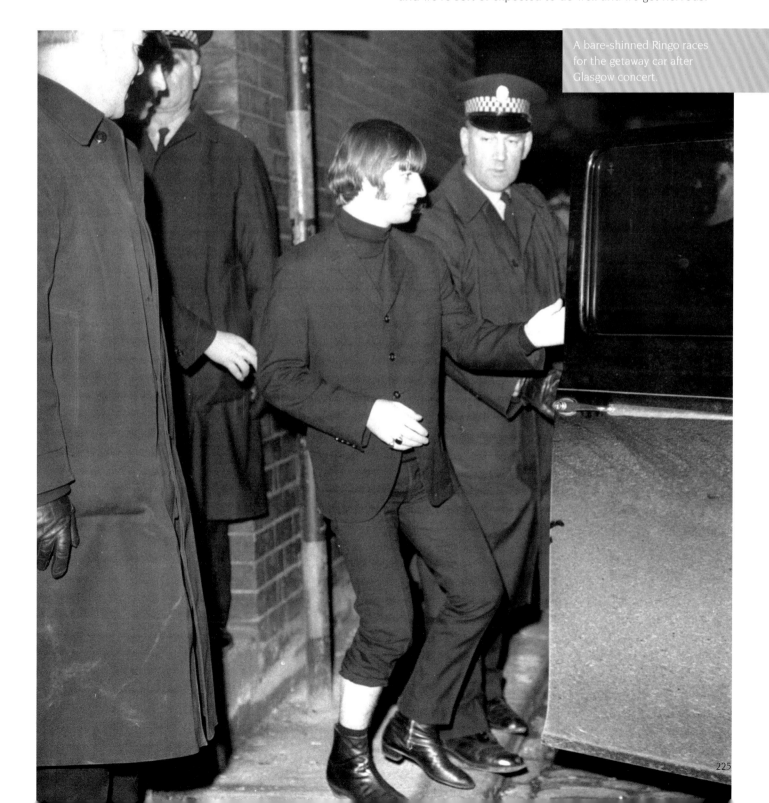

A bare-shinned Ringo races for the getaway car after Glasgow concert.

225

Something of a family affair, backstage visitors at the Empire included George's and Ringo's parents, George's girlfriend Pattie Boyd, Bessie Braddock MP, and Jimmy Tarbuck. Two girls, Susan Hall and Josephine McQuaid, were handing out Save the Cavern leaflets when Paul saw them and invited them backstage to discuss their campaign. (The legendary venue needed costly repairs to its drainage system and was closed by the City Council the following February. It was reopened in a blaze of publicity by Harold Wilson on 23rd July 1966 but eventually closed for good in 1973 and was demolished shortly thereafter. A modern re-creation now stands a few feet further down from the original site.)

Mr and Mrs Harrison, with Pattie Boyd (centre), at the Empire.

Paul backstage at Liverpool Empire with 'Save the Cavern' campaigners.

Tuesday 7th December

ABC Cinema, Ardwick, Manchester

After a day off in Liverpool, the drive to Manchester was taken at a snail's pace due to heavy fog, resulting in the Beatles arriving 12 minutes after showtime. An extra intermission was inserted while the group changed and dashed on to the stage. Also, while in Manchester, United Artists producer Walter Shenson met the Beatles to discuss ideas for their never-realized third film with Dick Lester.

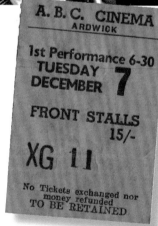

A.B.C. CINEMA
ARDWICK

1st Performance 6-30
TUESDAY
DECEMBER 7

FRONT STALLS
15/-

XG 11

No Tickets exchanged nor money refunded
TO BE RETAINED

A bored-looking Beatles watch TV in their dressing room at the Birmingham Odeon, 12th December.

Sunday 12th December

Capitol Theatre, Cardiff, Wales

The final night of the tour. To emphasize how the Beatles' popularity remained undiminished, 25,000 applications poured in for only 5,000 available seats at Cardiff, resulting in the theatre manager, Mr Bill Hall and three of his staff taking three days to return £12,000 to disappointed fans after all seats for the two shows had been allocated.

CAPITOL - CARDIFF

ARTHUR HOWES in association with BRIAN EPSTEIN presents

THE BEATLES

1st Performance at 5-30 p.m.

SUNDAY DECEMBER 12

DRESS CIRCLE 15/-

BLOCK C   F53

No ticket exchanged nor money refunded

THIS PORTION TO BE RETAINED

229

Tomorrow
Never Knows

1966

"*I think we can go on as the Beatles for as long as we want to, writing songs, making records. We're still developing...*
We've had all the ego bit, all about wanting to be remembered. We couldn't do any better than we've done already, could we?"

Paul McCartney,
The Sunday Times, 1966

With the benefit of hindsight 1966 proved to be a decisive year for the Beatles. Having achieved an unimaginable degree of popularity, the group resolved to give up live appearances – an unthinkable move that would end the career of any lesser artist in the Sixties and an act that came less than three years after the Beatles' triumphant appearance at the London Palladium.

The Beatles had grown as individuals, and their growing artistry and ever-broadening quest for knowledge had made Beatlemania seem increasingly archaic. Lennon, in particular, felt his natural artistic impulses were stifled by his "Beatle John" image. "Songs like 'Eight Days A Week' and 'She Loves You' sound like big drags to me now," he candidly told *Music Maker* magazine. "I turn the radio off if they're ever on."

"I've changed a lot over the past two years," George confirmed to Alan Smith of the *New Musical Express* in June. "I've realized that the Beatle bit is only a small part of myself and I try to keep it in perspective. I've increasingly become aware that there are other things in life than being a Beatle."

"I'd hate for us to be remembered for one or two things we seem to be getting remembered for now," Paul declared to Ray Coleman in rival pop paper *Disc & Music Echo* the same month. "I don't like our American image, for instance. I'd hate the Beatles to be remembered as four jovial mop tops, four silly little puppets, which is what Americans tend to think of us sometimes. If it's possible I'd like us to be remembered, when we're dead, as four people who made music that stands up to being remembered."

After the less than rapturous response to *Help!* (including a lukewarm review in the *Daily Mirror*) the Beatles were no longer happy to play caricatures of themselves – a script for a third Beatles film, A *Talent For Loving*, a Western based on the novel by Richard Condon, that was due to start shooting in April had been rejected and was permanently shelved.

The 7th January issue of the NME reported that Brian Epstein had flown to New York to negotiate another US tour for the Beatles, which the paper confirmed in March, as well as their first and only tours of Germany and Japan.

For the first half of the year the Beatles effectively vanished from the public eye, the biggest news event surrounding them being George's marriage to Pattie Boyd on 21st January, although in March, British fans could savour *The Beatles At Shea Stadium*, the television film made of the group's epoch-making performance the previous August. The April issue of *Beatles Monthly* ran a story that the Beatles might fly to Memphis on 11th April to record their new single, with George Martin accompanying them. With the group all being lovers of the Stax sound of Otis Redding, Wilson Pickett and the label's

other great soul singers, the Beatles were looking to get the same deep sound that they heard on these imported American recordings. The trip never occurred and the Beatles were back at EMI on 6th April to commence 10 weeks of recording in the midst of which, on 1st May, they performed their last-ever British concert at the NME Poll Winners Concert before 10,000, although the appearance was not announced as such.

The first result from the Beatles time in the studio, 'Paperback Writer' / 'Rain', was released on 10th June. Commentators were quick to seize on the fact that the record broke with Beatles tradition of entering the singles charts straight in at No. 1 during the first week (although it did eventually reach the pole position).

Thursday 23rd June

5

Having just completed their most artistically challenging album to date in *Revolver* (released 5th August), which contained songs that could no longer easily fit the Beatles' traditional two guitar, bass and drums live set-up, the Beatles reluctantly set out from London Airport on BEA Flight 502 at 11.05am for their last world tour, taking in Germany, Japan and the Philippines.

Set-list: 'Rock And Roll Music', 'She's A Woman', 'If I Needed Someone', 'Day Tripper', 'Baby's In Black', 'I Feel Fine', 'Yesterday', 'I Wanna Be Your Man', 'Nowhere Man', 'Paperback Writer' and 'I'm Down'.

Support acts on the German leg were Cliff Bennett and the Rebel Rousers, Peter and Gordon and local group, the Rattles.

The three-day German tour, with concerts in Munich, Essen and a nostalgic return to Hamburg, passed without incident although the police were often brutal in handling the crowds. It was also painfully obvious that the Beatles had barely rehearsed and after six months off stage, were dreadfully ramshackle as a live act.

The Beatles depart London for Munich, 23rd June.

The Beatles arrive in Tokyo,
30th June.

THE ✠ BEATLES

A

ビートルズ　7月2日《土》　6:30開演 // 日本武道館

主催＝読売新聞社・中部日本放送
協賛＝ライオン歯磨・ライオン油脂　／　後援＝日本航空・東芝音楽工業

2,100
7/2
土6:30

裏面に住所・氏名をお書き下さい。
次の音楽会のお知らせをさしあげます。

扉　　階　　列　　番

The Beatles onstage at the
Tokyo Budokan, 30th June.

The Beatles at Tokyo press conference, 30th June.

In Japan, this barely mattered as the Beatles were treated like royal emissaries, guarded by a security force totaling an incredible 35,000, from the moment they landed in Tokyo during the early hours of 30th June. Over 200,000 had applied for tickets for the 33,000 seats for three shows at the Nippon Budokan Hall so extra matinees were added on 1st and 2nd July. There had been threats from Japanese extremists that the Beatles were defiling the sacred venue – traditionally, a judo hall. The clinical, though appreciative, reception the group received only served to expose their musical inadequacies: forgotten words, off-key harmonies and often out of tune instrumentation.

Reaching Manila, the Beatles performed what should have been two triumphant major outdoor concerts at the Rizal Stadium on 4th July before nearly 100,000 people. However, this was totally overshadowed by the Beatles unintentionally slighting the first lady, Imelda Marcos, by not turning up to a state reception held in their honour at the presidential palace. The Beatles' press representative, Tony Barrow, attempted to apologize, explaining that the invitation had never been received, but this failed to alleviate the situation. The local television news and press were full of the story and for the first time in their travels, the Beatles were in a serious situation where their physical well-being was at risk. The following day, the group's security was withdrawn, leaving them to make their own way to the airport where they were jostled and jeered at.

This terrifying experience only made the decision to retreat from the concert stage easier for John Lennon and, particularly, George Harrison. Although all of the Beatles were still in their early to mid-twenties, Harrison later remarked how the pressures of Beatlemania seemed to make them age faster than ordinary mortals.

When interviewed on their return to Britain, he only half-jokingly remarked, "Now we are going to have a couple of weeks to recuperate before we go and get beaten up in America."

'I thought it was the usual police escort'

DAILY MIRROR, Wednesday, July 6, 1966   PAGE 13

BEATLES, GO HOME!

That was the chant as an airport crowd jostled and jeered the boys in 'snub' row

One of the Beatles' party, Alf Bicknell, is helped up after a fall caused by a kick on the leg.

NEVER before has anything remotely like this happened to the Beatles.

Up to yesterday, they could be called the most feted young men in the world, acclaimed with frenzied enthusiasm wherever they went.

Yesterday there was frenzy . . . but of anger and hate.

The Beatles were jostled, booed and jeered in a hectic airport scene at Manila, capital of the Philippines, as they left for their homeward trip by way of New Delhi.

Fists were shaken at them. Screwed-up pieces of paper were thrown at them.

And there were shouts of "Beatles, Go Home!" . . . "Go to Hell!" . . . "Get out of our country!" . . . and "We don't want you here!"

About 200 angry Filipinos — young and old — staged this unprecedented demonstration against the Beatles. They were smarting under an alleged snub to Senora Imelda Marcos, wife of their President.

Many Filipinos, including the Press, were upset when John, Ringo, Paul and George failed to appear as invited to meet Senora Marcos at the palace on Monday.

Regrets

The Beatles said that they knew nothing about the invitation.

And last night the President and his wife issued a statement regretting the airport incidents.

They added: "There was no intention on the part of the Beatles to slight the first lady or the Government."

But, earlier, the crowd at the airport had thought otherwise.

After the Beatles arrival at the airport, an angry crowd grew round them. Within minutes people were pushing them.

One of the party, Alf Bicknell, fell after being kicked in the leg.

A radio reporter who got near the Beatles said that a Filipino swung a wild right at Ringo Starr—but missed. By contrast with their arrival, the departure of the Beatles was officially brusque and without any VIP treatment.

The group had to carry their baggage up to the second floor themselves. The power for the airport escalator had been turned off.

Almost all police protection and special arrangements were cancelled—and the tax office announced that the Beatles could not leave the Philippines until they had made a declaration of their earnings.

The Beatles themselves were bewildered. As they walked to their airliner, Paul McCartney exclaimed disconsolately:

THEY TREATED US LIKE ANIMALS, SAYS RINGO

A bewildering moment . . . reflected in the expression of John Lennon (in the background, right) amid a jostling crowd. Ringo Starr is in the foreground — and on the left is the Beatles' road manager, Neil Aspinall.

"Man, I don't understand!"

CONSOLATION awaited the Beatles in a tumultuous and joyous welcome at New Delhi airport last night. Again they were pushed, shoved and pelted —but with garlands.

"They treated us like animals where we just came from," Ringo Starr told 600 Indian fans.

"We never meant to upset anybody by not attending the party. It was all fixed up for us to go—but the only thing was that nobody told us."

John gets a mobbing of a more loving kind while leaving London Airport after the Manila incident, 8th July.

Friday 8th July 5

The Beatles returned to London Airport at 6am after a two-day stop in New Delhi, India, where George continued his fascination with Indian music. The British press were naturally keen to hear about the Beatles' frightening experience in Manila.

Paul: "*We got put into the airport transit lounge and then we got pushed around from one corner of the lounge to another, and they started knocking over our road managers... I swear there was about 30 of them doing the kicking and booing...*"

John: "*No plane's going to go through the Philippines with me on it. I wouldn't even fly over it.*"

The Manila experience left Brian Epstein a nervous wreck as the Beatles held him responsible. Shortly after arriving back in London Epstein was confined to bed for 10 days with an attack of glandular fever, forcing the postponement of an American trip to prepare for the Beatles' forthcoming tour there. However, he was forced to leave the Welsh village of Portmeirion, where he had gone to recover, to fly to New York

tour would be cancelled.

The preposterous furore that blew up in the wake of John's off-the-cuff remarks only strengthened the Beatles' resolve to give up live shows. In the meantime, a total of 22 Southern

to defend the latest controversy involving his charges.

Back in March, as part of a four-part Beatles series for the London *Evening Standard*, John had given an in-depth interview on various topics to journalist Maureen Cleave, who also happened to be a friend, hence its unguarded nature. When asked about religion, he casually remarked that due to the lessening influence of the Church, he thought the Beatles' influence was more popular than Christ. Having just read Hugh J. Schonfield's *The Passover Plot*, he added, "Jesus was alright. It's his disciples who were thick and ordinary that ruins it for me."

The remarks buried deep within the piece caused barely a ripple in Britain but when the article was reprinted in America for the teen magazine *Datebook* and the Jesus remark was taken out of context and used as a leading quote, the infamous uproar it attracted was instant. Demonstrations and protests were widespread enough for the tour organizers to be concerned about the Beatles' safety, hastening Epstein's arrival in New York to state that John's comments had been taken out of context and to deny rumours that the radio stations in the Bible Belt area refused to play their records and organized Beatle bonfires. In scenes reminiscent of Ray Bradbury's *Farenheit* 451, stacks of Beatles' records, books and photos were burned in public demonstrations.

The right-wing Ku Klux Klan threatened to picket the show in Memphis. Having only just experienced clear and present danger in the Philippines, it was against this backdrop that the Beatles prepared for their final tour.

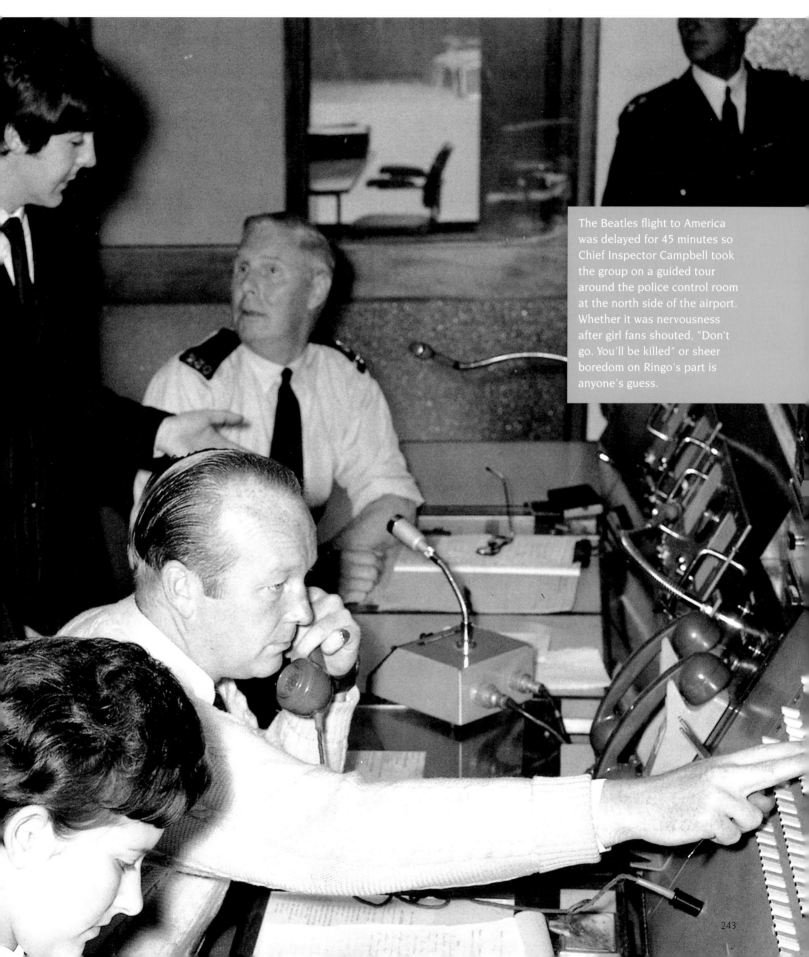

The Beatles flight to America was delayed for 45 minutes so Chief Inspector Campbell took the group on a guided tour around the police control room at the north side of the airport. Whether it was nervousness after girl fans shouted, "Don't go. You'll be killed" or sheer boredom on Ringo's part is anyone's guess.

Thursday 11th August

Against a "no interviews" request to waiting media, the Beatles left London Airport for America as a group for the last time, travelling to Chicago to start the tour at the International Amphitheatre on 12th August. Their original reservations, booked three weeks earlier, were cancelled by TWA because of the current nationwide airline strike in America. The Beatles entourage instead were switched to a Pan-Am flight to Chicago via a brief stopover in Boston.

Arriving in Chicago at 4.18 local time at the Astor Towers Hotel, all eyes were on John as he made several attempts to explain his original comments until being forced into making an apology. John's clarification was accepted by most who'd been offended, including Alabama station WAQY which lifted its boycott on Beatles discs. However, as the tour progressed, the Beatles were fully aware of how vulnerable they were to extremists. As Paul said, "If they'd wanted to shoot us, it would have been easy for them, at one of those concerts with thousands of people milling around." Further fuel was added to the fire when, during a press conference at New York's Warwick Hotel, both John and George came out against the Vietnam War, something they had been advized by Brian Epstein not to remark upon. Despite the unwarranted controversy, the Beatles' popularity remained unaffected if the latest ticket and record sales statistics were anything to go by, although filling maximum capacity at the huge baseball stadiums the Beatles were booked into was no longer a given. In Los Angeles, 45,000 tickets for a show at Dodger Stadium on 28th August went on the day of sale but a return to Shea Stadium left some 10,000 seats unsold.

On 29th August, the Beatles played their last-ever live show before an audience of 25,000 at San Francisco's Candlestick Park. On the plane taking the entourage back to Los Angeles after the concert, George Harrison formally declared, "Well, that's it, I'm not a Beatle anymore." His decisive comment meant no longer having to endure tedious press conferences and perform on concert stages where the music was secondary to the event – "tribal rites" as John Lennon memorably described them.

The Beatles arrived back at London Airport on Wednesday 31st August with touring finally behind them. Each of the four

followed individual pursuits; John flew to Germany on 5th September to start filming his role in Dick Lester's anti-war black comedy, *How I Won The War*; Paul wrote the music to the Boulting Brothers' Northern comedy *The Family Way* and went off on safari (accompanied by Mal Evans) to Kenya; George spent a month in India studying the sitar under Ravi Shankar's tutelage; and Ringo stayed at home, enjoying domesticity with his family.

With the Beatles inactive and rumours flying that the group were no longer, Brian Epstein felt compelled to make a statement: "There's no real question of the Beatles retiring. Let's face it, what is happening at the moment is that they're simmering down. Making films, writing music, making records … that's their future."

An apprehensive Epstein still laboured under the belief that he could talk "the boys" round to doing a concert tour of Britain before the year was out. But the group were adamant. Brian threw himself into other business ventures but with the Beatles no longer interested in making personal appearances, he felt his management role (at least in the way it had been) was less assured.

For the first time, much to EMI's chagrin, the Beatles no longer felt bound by the remarkable annual two albums, three singles product rate that had passed for the norm.

Now, days, sometimes weeks, would be spent on just one song if they so desired.

"Everything we've done so far has been rubbish, as I see it today," George told the *Mirror* in an interview published 11th November. "It doesn't mean a thing to what we want to do now."

And so it was, the Beatles reconvened in late November to start work on the brilliant 'Strawberry Fields Forever' / 'Penny Lane' single and *Sgt. Pepper's Lonely Heart's Club Band* – a concentrated bout of creativity that could not (and would not) be interrupted by the demands of "being Beatles". Even the group's changing appearance – sprouting moustaches, colourful garb and John donning National Health specs – seemed like a conscious break from their previous guise of matching moptops. However, without the bonding that touring engendered, the ties that bound the Beatles together would slowly unwind until the group's disintegration was all but inevitable.

"I was too scared to break away from the Beatles," John Lennon recalled to *Playboy* magazine in 1980, "but I'd been looking to it since '65 [*sic*] when we stopped touring… And so from '65 on I was sort of vaguely looking for somewhere to go, but I didn't really have the nerve to really step in the boat by myself and push the boat off."

DAILY MIRROR, Friday, November 11, 1966   PAGE 9

JOHN—in film role

RINGO—with gimmick glasses

AT THE CROSSROADS

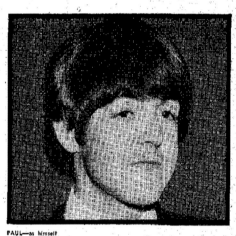

PAUL—as himself

● Everything we've done so far has been rubbish ●

GEORGE HARRISON, Nov. 10, 1966

GEORGE—with new moustache

THE BEATLES talk to DON SHORT

THERE'S no great mystery, says John Lennon, about the long, long silence of the Beatles.

It's just what the others are making out of it, says George Harrison.

For weeks their marked absence from show business life has led to mounting predictions of a split-up of the world's most famous foursome.

And now the Beatles have realised it's all gone beyond a joke.

But the answer seems quite simple.

They are at the crossroads. And it's something Paul, John, George and Ringo have got to sort out for themselves.

They don't want to do any further tours at home or abroad because the value of such tours "is not progressive."

THE Beatles are exploring . . . trying to find their own new horizon.

BUT THEY ARE NOT GOING TO SPLIT UP.

Endlessly they experiment with new sounds and they still haven't finally settled on a screen play for their next film—twice postponed because they've been cautious about choosing the right subject.

Time has slipped by. But now, as questions press about their future, the Beatles are going to brush away the cobwebs.

They plan a new single and another LP before their film.

Said George Harrison: "We've been resting and thinking. It gave us a chance to re-assess things.

Real

"After all, we've had four years doing what everybody else wanted us to do.

"Now we're doing what we want to do. . . .

"But whatever we do it has got to be real and progressive.

"Everything we've done so far has been rubbish as I see it today. Other people may like what we've done, but we're not kidding ourselves.

"It doesn't mean a thing to what we want to do now."

George continued: "People live too easily in a plastic world.

"They think they are doing something, but when they peg out—they've done nothing."

John Lennon grinned: "George is being a bit blunt.

"You can always look back and say what you've done before was rubbish. Especially in comparison with what you're doing today.

"It was all vital at the time, even if it looks daft when you see things differently later on."

DID this mean they were ashamed of their earlier songs like "She Loves You"? . . .

John shook his head: "I think of that particular song as a childhood memory."

Then the Beatles talked about the rumours.

John told me: "We've no intention of splitting up. We're always going to be recording."

And tours? "No one has said anything definite about them," said John, "but with the film and everything else on we're not going to have much chance for some time. We've got to give all our energy to the film.

"We've got to be tight, otherwise find ourselves doing 'Help!' all over again."

Those splitting-up rumours stemmed largely, the Beatles admit themselves, from their own independent interests.

Offer

GEORGE has just returned from a six-week course on the sitar in India;

JOHN has been playing a soldier in a new Dick Lester comedy picture;

PAUL has been scoring the theme music for Hayley Mills's next picture;

RINGO has been busy—just being Ringo.

"From our independent experiences we've each got something more to offer," said John.

And George added: "The thing is that we haven't been worrying ourselves. It's all the others who've been doing the worrying for us.

"It's a laugh.

"If we ever did split, we wouldn't split as people. We would still be good buddy pals," said John.

"It isn't the money. They told us a bit back that we needn't work again if we didn't want to. But you can't really stop—it's all the interest and that kind of thing."

Has there been a row with their manager, Brian Epstein, as a lot of people are saying?

"Row with Eppy? Not us," said George.

Said Mr. Epstein: "There have been no rows at all. We have always seen eye to eye."

But he was obviously anxious over the growing rumours about the Beatles' future.

FANS besieged Mr. Epstein's Belgravia home last weekend demanding another Beatles tour, but he said:

"I am not at all sure that personal appearances are in their best interests, but that doesn't mean they will never appear in person again. They will."

Certain

He added: "I don't think they will split up because I'm certain that they will want to do things together for a long long time."

Which left Mr. Lennon to joke with resignation: "I suppose that means we have got to be four mop-tops again!"

And In The End...

"We were just a band who made it very, very big – that's all"

John Lennon,
Rolling Stone, 1970

From 1966 until the Beatles official demise in 1970 fans held out hope that the Beatles would perform together on stage again. Periodically, stories emerged that the group had been offered a huge amount to this effect – most notably in October 1967, when Sid Bernstein, the promoter of the Beatles' fantastically successful concerts at Shea Stadium, tabled an offer of one million dollars for a return to the site of previous triumphs. But, as John Lennon told Ray Coleman of *Disc & Music Echo*, "How can we tour like we used to? We can't… We could send out four waxwork dummies of ourselves and let them stand on stage and probably make another million quid, but we don't want it."

The idea of a live concert in 1967 was anathema to the Beatles, who were well immersed in their recording phase. They could now freely use the studio as an ideas workshop – experimenting with the sounds heard in their heads with George Martin ready to translate them onto tape. With Lennon withdrawing into himself, and Harrison smitten with Indian philosophy, it was McCartney who appeared to take over the Beatles direction after the unexpected death of manager Brian Epstein in August that year from an accidental overdose. It was also Paul who most pushed that the Beatles should consider playing live again – concerts being the lifeblood of any successful artist.

After the ornate flourishes of landmark album *Sgt. Pepper's Lonely Hearts Club Band*, the lengthy sessions for what became *The Beatles* (or the double 'White Album' as it's widely known) had moved the band's sound back to basics on such tracks as 'Back In The USSR, 'Birthday' and 'Yer Blues' – songs that could potentially be reproduced live without too much difficulty. Successful events like the Monterey International Pop Festival of June '67 (for which McCartney was on the Board of Directors) had demonstrated how times had changed in presenting live pop (or as it was now being increasingly called, rock) music, meaning an act of the Beatles' stature could now be heard and appreciated thanks to more sophisticated sound systems, unlike what seemed like only yesterday when the Beatles battled to be heard through inadequate PAs to distant, deafening Beatlemaniacs.

It's interesting that at roughly the same time the Beatles eschewed live appearances their closest contemporaries also temporarily brought performing to a halt. In the summer of 1965, Bob Dylan had outraged his folk purist audience by welding his inventive lyricism to loud rock 'n' roll – in many ways, influenced by British groups like the Beatles. Having toured for a year with an electric band The Hawks (later becoming The Band), Dylan suffered a motorbike accident in July 1966 near his home in

upstate New York and did not perform officially onstage again for three years – making the homespun 'Basement Tapes' at the Band's 'Big Pink' home in Woodstock.

Within a year of their formation in 1962, the Rolling Stones started to tour continuously, playing around Britain, Europe, Australia and America, in venues ranging from ballrooms to state fairs on a punishing schedule the equal, if not more arduous, than that undertaken by the Beatles. Yet after a final swing around Britain in autumn 1966, the Stones retreated into Olympic Studios in London for a protracted series of recording sessions, broken only by a riotous European tour and appearances in court for drug offences over the spring and summer of '67.

While both groups were close and shared a similar empathy, the Stones, "a blacker version of the Beatles" as Mick Jagger once described them, were still considered to be bona fide live performers, and their much touted return to the live stage in 1969 was considered a far more realistic prospect than the Fab Four re-entering the concert arena.

"I always felt that with the Beatles, performing wasn't really their forte when they were big," Jagger commented that year. *"Their forte was songwriting – ours was doing concerts."*
Keith Richards agreed. *"I think it's impossible for [the Beatles] to do a tour"*, he opined to Ritchie Yorke of *Rolling Stone*, *"Mick has said it before, but it's worth repeating… the Beatles are primarily a recording group. Even though they drew the biggest crowds of their era in North America, I think the Beatles had passed their performing peak even before they were famous."*
While partly concurring with Richards' view, John Lennon always felt resentful that the Stones' rebel image was deliberately played up by their manager Andrew Oldham while the Beatles were made more establishment friendly by Brian Epstein. *"[The Beatles] best work was never recorded…"* Lennon told *Rolling Stone* in 1970, *"We were performers in spite of what Mick says about us, in Liverpool, Hamburg and around the dance halls. What we generated was fantastic when we played straight rock, and there was nobody to touch us in Britain. But as soon as we made it, the edges were knocked off… we sold out. The music was dead before we even went on the [first] theatre tour of Britain."*

Despite the Beatles' immense fame and popularity, Paul McCartney never lost sight of the band's performing roots. He constantly enthused to the others his proposal of taking things back to the wellspring – of the Beatles returning full circle by playing humble gigs unannounced at small clubs and venues (something which Paul eventually achieved with

his band Wings in 1972). Following the release of *The Beatles* in November 1968, the Roundhouse, one of London's new alternative rock venues, holding 2,500, was chosen as a possible venue to stage the Beatles' live return. A competition to win tickets to watch the group rehearse and record an hour-long "live" TV show some time in January 1969 for worldwide broadcast ran in the December issue of the *Beatles Monthly* magazine.

Meanwhile, the Beatles moved on to a soundstage in Twickenham Film Studios on 2nd January to start rehearsals, being filmed for a documentary by director Michael Lindsay-Hogg, with still only a vague plan as to the end result. It soon became apparent that it was a case of too much, too soon after the bickering and tension that had characterized the protracted 'White Album' sessions. Lennon, newly under the spell of heroin, was barely contributing and left his say in proceedings to his artistic partner, Yoko Ono, a pernicious

(and constant) presence throughout. Having recently returned from America, where he had been accepted as a musical equal during informal jams with Bob Dylan and members of The Band, Harrison resented the hegemony exercised by McCartney, especially now as his writing was entering a particularly fertile patch. George also baulked at the idea of a live show in some of the exotic locations under consideration, including an ocean-going boat with an invited audience and a Roman amphitheatre in Tunisia.

With the atmosphere at an all-time low, only a week into the rehearsals, Harrison became the second Beatle to declare he was quitting (Ringo had been the first to temporarily walk out during the stressful 'White Album' sessions the previous summer). After several meetings, George agreed to return if all talk of a live show was abandoned. Instead, the rest of the filming would concentrate on the Beatles recording a new album in the basement studio of their Apple headquarters on

Savile Row. But still, hopeful talk of a live event continued and Lindsay-Hogg was anxious to get a climatic sequence to the hours of less than magical film he'd been overseeing, for what became Let It Be.

So it was that on Thursday, 30th January, Mal Evans and assistant Kevin Harrington carried the Beatles' equipment up the stairs of the Apple building at 3 Savile Row on to the rooftop where around lunchtime, the Beatles blasted out an impromptu 40 minute run-though of some of the songs they had been working on. The stray audience of office workers and curious passers-by, craning their necks upwards to try and hear where the music was coming from, had no way of knowing the significance of what they were witnessing – the last time the Beatles performed live, no matter how unorthodox the means. As the police terminated proceedings following noise complaints, John Lennon moved to his mike and famously jested, "I'd like to say thank you on behalf of the group and ourselves and I hope we passed the audition."

The Beatles had long ago passed the audition but were now four individuals facing a much more cynical, unforgiving world in the Seventies. Although each would go on to make successful solo recordings or in the case of Paul McCartney, undertake record-breaking tours with Wings and under his own name, the magic associated when all four parts of the whole were together was conspicuous by its absence. The Beatles had given so much in the Sixties and now they needed the space to grow as individuals.

But still people wouldn't let it lie. Throughout the Seventies, alongside headlines regarding the oil crisis, Nixon's resignation, and the three-day week, would be the latest "Beatles to reunite" story, including, by way of example, an attempt in 1976 by Los Angeles pop promoter Bill Sargent who offered a guaranteed $50m incentive for one reunion concert to be televised worldwide on closed circuit television. With no immediate response Sargent doubled his offer with an additional stake in the broadcast profits but still to no avail. A spokesman for McCartney, who was currently undertaking a highly successful American Wings tour, issued a terse "No comment!"

That same year, Sid Bernstein got in on the act – taking out a full-page ad in the New York Herald Tribune asking that the Beatles reunite for a one-off charity concert. But even a charitable appeal was equally in vain. As George Harrison commented at the time, "It's like putting the responsibility of making the world a nicer place on to the Beatles which I think is most unfair."

In an interview given to Playboy just weeks before his tragic death on 8th December 1980, which brought any serious

notion of a Beatles reunion to a sudden and definite halt, John Lennon said it best: "Talking about the Beatles getting back together is an illusion. That was 10 years ago. The Beatles exist only on film and record and in people's minds. You cannot get back together what no longer exists. We are not those four people anymore."

Rooftop Beatles upset the neighbours

THE Beatles put on a free lunchtime show yesterday. And, appropriately for young men at the top of their particular profession, they staged it on a rooftop. Unhappily, it didn't go down well with the neighbours.

The roof they chose was the one over their Apple headquarters in Savile-row, London, a thoroughfare where music is not generally regarded as one of the more fashionable occupations.

Indeed, the famous foursome had hardly sent the first amplified bars echoing down the street before the verdicts were being reached.

At the woollen merchants next door to Apple, director Stanley Davis said quite bluntly: "I want this noise stopped. You can't use a telephone, dictate a letter or have your window open."

Ringo's drums rolled. Paul McCartney's voice be2ned: "Don't let me down . . ." But Mr. Stephen King, chief accountant at the Royal Bank of Scotland—right opposite—was not a bit impressed.

He said: "I am furious.

By MIRROR REPORTER

We were trying to talk to our customers but couldn't hear them. I telephoned the police but apparently they are powerless to do anything."

Four policemen did arrive at the Apple building and two of them went in. But the 40-minute session continued, drawing crowds to the street and on to adjoining rooftops.

An Apple spokesman said later that the Beatles played "four or five numbers for a film they are making."

Now the neighbours are hoping to find a way to ensure that there will be no repeat performance.

Acknowledgments

The first individuals to be thanked are the Beatles themselves. As a child born in the '60s, theirs was the first music I was ever aware of, and therefore they are responsible for my ongoing fascination with the era. So thank you John, Paul, George and Ringo.

For their kind help and assistance: Andy Davis, Mark Lewisohn (whose eagerly awaited trilogy of *histories* on all things Fab looks set to be the definitive word), Chris Charlesworth, Mark 'Wag' Wagstaff, The British Newspaper Library, and all the folk at Mirrorpix.

Special thanks go to Don Short for sharing his Beatle memories in his splendid foreword and to Richard Havers for enthusiasm, patience and providing the opportunity.

Very special thanks to Pete Nash, chairman of the British Beatles Fan Club, who provided the memorabilia throughout this book. See www.britishbeatlesfanclub.co.uk for more up-to-date Beatles information.

Sources: *The Beatles Book Monthly, Disc Weekly, Disc & Music Echo, Melody Maker, New Musical Express, Record Mirror, The Beatles -* Hunter Davies (Heinemann 1968), *The Beatles Files -* Andy Davis (Bramley Books 1998), *The Beatles Live! -* Mark Lewisohn (Pavilion Books 1986), *The Complete Beatles Chronicle -* Mark Lewisohn (Pyramid Books 1992), *Lennon Remembers –* Jann S. Wenner (Verso 2000), *Last Interview: All We Are Saying – John Lennon & Yoko Ono -* David Sheff (Sidgwick & Jackson 2000), *Small Town Saturday Night -* Trevor Simpson (Milltown Memories 2007) and the various British regional and daily newspapers quoted from; foremost, of course, being the *Daily Mirror*.

A big hug and kiss to Felicia.